THE WOODHOUSES LETTERS

WHAT THEY REVEALED AND WHERE THEY LED

THE WOODHOUSES LETTERS

WHAT THEY REVEALED AND WHERE THEY LED

Studies of nineteenth century English justice

by

Eveline Barbara Dean

ROSS ANDERSON PUBLICATIONS

Published in 1986 by
Ross Anderson Publications Limited
Larkhill House
160 St. Georges Road
Bolton BL1 2PJ

British Library Cataloguing in Publication Data

Dean, Eveline Barbara
The Woodhouses letters: what they revealed and where they led: studies in nineteenth century English justice.
1. Law – England – History and criticism
2. Punishment – England – History – 19th century 3. Corrections – England – History – 19th century
I. Title
344.207′09′034 KD532

ISBN 0–86360–025–5

Photoset in Linotron Plantin by
Northern Phototypesetting Co., Bolton
Printed in Great Britain by
Billings of Worcester

CONTENTS

ACKNOWLEDGMENTS

My first thanks must go to the late Agnes Stansfield without whose help this book could not have been written. She it was who introduced me to the old letters and papers which her mother had found years earlier in their family home at Woodhouses, near Ashton-under-Lyne, and she allowed me to take and keep them while I was working on this book. It is sad that she did not live to see the book in print, but she read the manuscript in its final form and had checked the details concerning her family. According to her wish the *Woodhouses Letters* have now been given to Chetham's Library, Manchester, and it is with the permission of the feoffees of Chetham's Library that I have quoted from them.

I am grateful for the help given by the staff of the Public Record Office when I worked on documents at Chancery Lane and Kew, and I acknowledge also the help of the Cheshire Record Office and of the Archives Office of Tasmania. I have worked happily in many libraries and have appreciated the willing efforts of their staff. Particularly I must mention the Leicester University Library where, through the kindness of the librarian in allowing me full facilities, I have had access to law reports and legal literature. I have also received help from the State Library of Tasmania and from the Public Library in Norfolk Island.

Members of my family have given support, and I thank especially my nephew Christopher Dean for his assistance and my mother for her unfailing help and inspiration from the beginning of my work to its end.

Research is endless, and it is not unlikely that the work of others may yet produce new evidence or modify some of my findings. An article by Mrs Heather Coutie in *Cheshire History* No. 14 recently introduced me to two documents I had not previously seen. They are fuller copies of the supposed pedigree of Edmund Davenport and must have been sent about 1846 to the representatives of two families of Cheshire gentry, both near neighbours of the Davenports of Bramhall. There is the signature on one document of 'Giles Powell', the friend who, according to Edmund Davenport's last letter, was searching records on his behalf. This pedigree reveals the marriage of Thomas Davenport on which Edmund then relied to prove his descent. It is a marriage I had already considered and written off as almost certainly not that of Thomas of Bramhall. It makes Edmund's claim all the thinner, but I think we must accept the fact that he sincerely believed in it. One could easily be mistaken genealogically when pieces of evidence were unco-ordinated and difficult to find.

There are still many unanswered questions but, right or wrong, the case of Edmund Davenport has proved an absorbing study. I have tried to see him as a person and to portray his unhappy career, together with that of his contemporary J. K. Winterbottom, in its human setting.

April, 1986 E.B.D.

ILLUSTRATIONS

To the memory of
Agnes Stansfield

I
THE MEETING TIME

Each Saturday night when from labour we'r freed
Of news both domestic and foreign to read
To Dyson's we hie where good cheer's to be found
And mirth and good humour gose merrily round
. . . . . .

As clear distinct reading we love to enjoy
In that usefull task we our Landlord employ
Whose accents and emphasis pleasingly sound
And knowledge and humour at Dyson's is found
The reading being over then each tells his tale
As opinion or humour or whim may prevail
and the goke [joke] and the glass passes merrily round
For mirth and good humour at Dyson's abound
. . . . . .

Though heat in debates we some times may perceive
With pleasure we always forget and forgive
And in our opinions to nothing we'r bound
For freedom's true standard at Dyson's is found
. . . . . .

The fireside statesman or prattlering nave
May pertend to be wise may pertend to be brave
We laugh at his folly enjoy the vague sound
And mirth and good humour at Dyson's gose round
. . . . . .

Should Radical blackguards attempt to invade
This peaceful retreat from the toils of our Trade
By the strength of our Landlord the street he'll soon find
And leave parkling mirth and good humour behind
Though the cold chilling blasts of December may blow
And the tempest be heaping its mountains of snow
Our Landlord's good fire spreads cheerfulness round
And mirth and good humour at Dyson's abound

From the *Woodhouses Letters*

This poem (or piece of doggerel) came to light in a bundle of old letters and papers approximately one hundred years after it was written. It was found in an old farmhouse in Woodhouses, near Ashton-under-Lyne, and it forms, I think, a key to the understanding of the collection of letters which was with it, and which I have called the *Woodhouses Letters*. It is written in a firm hand on three sides of a double sheet of paper, and it has been folded and addressed to 'Mr Dyson, Inn Keeper, Hooley Hill', with the inscription 'The Meeting Time'. There is a signature, 'Geo. Webster', presumably that of the author. Four verses of the 'poem' have been omitted in this printed version, for they contain words now indecipherable, but they do show that memories of the Napoleonic wars and of George IV's treatment of his queen were still fresh in the writer's mind. These details date the composition as belonging to the 1820s or early 1830s, probably earlier than most of the other letters and papers in the collection and certainly before Queen Victoria came to the throne, for, declares one of the omitted lines,

> Like good loyal subjects we'll drink to our King.

There are other papers in the collection which are in George Webster's handwriting. He would seem to have been the most literate of the little group of friends which assembled every Saturday evening at Dyson's in Hooley Hill. This hamlet was situated about two miles south of Ashton-under-Lyne between the west bank of the river Tame and the main Stockport road, where now is the railway station of Guide Bridge. It had sprung up in the late eighteenth century with the development of a hat manufactory there, and it is not surprising to find that several of the friends mentioned in the *Woodhouses Letters* were hatters. George Webster, the author of the poem, was a hatter. He lived in Dukinfield, in 'Ollerenshaw's Buildings', a row or group of dwellings housing about thirty families, on 'Furnace Hill', a district of recently-established cotton mills. William Harrop and John Dyson (perhaps the son of the innkeeper) were also hatters living in Hooley Hill, but John Swindells was far distant at *The Brickmaker's Arms* on Rochdale Road, Manchester. The person who, I believe, inspired this collection of letters, lived a few miles away in the hamlet of Woodhouses. He was William Davenport (called 'Will'), who had moved to Woodhouses from

Stansfield Fold (previously Andrew's Fold), c.1920 (*Estate of the late Miss Agnes Stansfield*)

Blackley, the village north of Manchester where he was born. Like the rest of his family Will was a handloom weaver, though not now in cotton. Silk weaving was the speciality of Woodhouses and, as this was a finer type of work than the weaving of cottons, less easily undertaken by machinery, it is possible that Will Davenport was in a slightly less precarious financial position than the relatives he had left behind in Blackley.

Will firmly believed in his family's claim to be heirs to a rich estate in north east Cheshire. We can imagine the close-knit company at Dyson's, where every man could 'tell his tale', finding Will Davenport's affairs and the claims of his family to wealth and property an entrancing topic. When in 1829 the line at Bramhall died out, Will watched the attempts of his older cousin Edmund to establish himself as the rightful heir, and by the middle and late 1830s, when Edmund was in prison and could do no more, Will became personally active. The years between 1837 and 1842 were a time of acute depression and hardship in the industrial areas of South Lancashire, and dire need could have spurred on Will and his friends to their greatest efforts during these years. Will collected correspondence concerning Edmund's case. He accumulated letters covering the years 1829 to 1846, commencing with a short note and account from a London solicitor transferring Edmund's legal work to a Manchester firm, and ending with a letter from Edmund Davenport to his daughter. Will's friends wrote and received letters concerning births, marriages and deaths of members of the Davenport family, and they searched for wills and inquisitions. At a time when 'family history' was the monopoly of the rich, and the documents pertaining to it difficult of access, these amateur genealogists attempted to trace Will's ancestry for hundreds of years, and especially they tried to trace the seventeenth century 'missing link'. Of course they had an object in view, for all would hope to share ultimately in Will's family's good fortune.

One of them – some person unknown – went to London to the offices of the Court of Chancery for information about Edmund's chancery suit. This person was instructed, 'You will in the first Instance have to Inquire for the Bill of Discovery Davenport v Humphrys [sic]', and then he was advised, 'I would not ask persons that soliciet Employment but ask some respectable Door keeper when the office closes and make an appointment to see him at that time and Endeavour to get some useful Information from him Note the Clerks of the office are in the nature of Attorneys of the Court and I fancy you may get one of them to do your Business for you'.[1] Some success must have attended this mission, for George Webster wrote a memorandum showing a clear grasp of the principles underlying Edmund Davenport's chancery suit. At some other time John Swindells and Will Davenport, and later George Webster, visited the Manchester solicitors who had acted for Edmund in his common law ejectment case, and they saw documents concerning the case. George Webster was the man to interpret the legal and historical evidence. He it was who obtained the history of the Davenport family of Cheshire as it was given in the first (1819) edition of Ormerod's monumental *History of Cheshire*, and he delved into mediaeval ideas of land ownership, grants, inquisitions, wills and other legal matters. Some of Webster's ideas are wide open to criticism, but when we remember the archaic state of the land law in the early nineteenth century we can only marvel that a working-class man displayed such a grasp of its complexities.

Will, who was about fifty years of age when most of this activity took place, was not greatly literate himself, and he did not keep the letters and papers in his own little cottage. He gave them to his friend Rob Andrew to store. Robert Andrew was a farmer, and on a somewhat higher level in the social scale than Will Davenport. He lived in an ancient farmhouse at the southern edge of the hamlet of Woodhouses, and he, I think, acted as Will's business manager. When John Swindells and Will Davenport visited the solicitor's office in Manchester they were promised relevant documents at a later date, and Swindells wrote to George Webster to accompany him on that important expedition, saying, 'Can you get £1 0 0 [one pound] of Rob Andrew and be at our House on monday morning Next 8 OClock and you and me Can have Evrey Information'.[2] It was Rob Andrew who provided the finance to help affairs along, as well as taking custody of the correspondence. This letter, too, joined the store in his farmhouse!

Will Davenport collected all the letters he could lay hands on concerning the doings of his cousin Edmund. Letters from Edmund to family and friends found their way into Rob Andrew's farmhouse, and so too did a long series of letters addressed to Hugh Knowles, Edmund's representative in Bramhall during the months preceding the hearing of his ejectment case. They covered the year 1834 and the early part of 1835. Many of the letters were written to Knowles by John Ham, a man sent out from London on Edmund's business; others were from Edmund's friends and accredited agents, Thomas Sharpe and Peter Morrison. Besides being interested in his cousin Edmund's claim, Will was also interested in the claim of his more distant cousin Richard, and papers concerning Richard's case joined the others in Will's collection. Richard was a member of the family who still remained at Blackley, the home of these Davenports, and like the others he was a weaver. There was rivalry between Richard and Edmund concerning their exact places in the hierarchy of the Davenport family of Blackley, and Will obtained from Richard a copy of the family tree showing (so Richard believed) his descent. The disagreement of the cousins centred on the marriage of the first Samuel Davenport of Blackley – the first member of the family to settle in the village – and on the identity of his first-born son, both claiming this son to be *his* great-grandfather. Neither pedigree can now be fully proved from the registers, but Richard's appears to have the greater credibility.

Richard Davenport was one of that depressed class of cotton handloom weavers who by the end of the 1830s was facing starvation, and some time in 1839 or at the beginning of 1840 he decided to go forward with his case, poverty spurring him on. George Webster either wrote for him, or copied out for Will, a rather sad letter to someone unknown, pleading for legal help. The letter was put with the others on Rob Andrew's pile.

> Sir [it commenced], I write in the name and on behalf of Richard Davenport of Blackley in the County of Lancaster who humble Begs your pardon for persuming to trouble you with our affair But necessity must be our plea for a long Continued Bad Trade has Brought us to the last stage of Poverty.[3]

Richard was not a young man, and these were the very worst of the years for the cotton handloom weavers. He did receive some

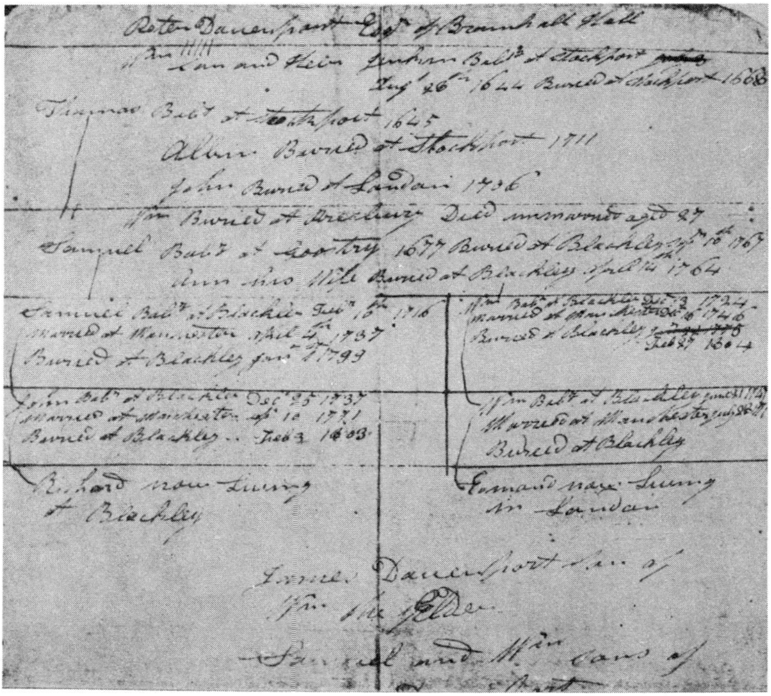

Peter Davenport Esq of Bramhall Hall

Wm Son and Heir [illegible] Bapt at Stockport Aug 26th 1644 Buried at Stockport 1668

Thomas Bapt at Stockport 1645

Albin Buried at Stockport 1711

John Buried at London 1736

Wm Buried at Blackley Died unmarried aged 87

Samuel Bapt at Coventry 1677 Buried at Blackley Apr 10th 1767

Ann his Wife Buried at Blackley April 14th 1764

Samuel Bapt at Blackley Dec 15th 1716 Married at Manchester April 2nd 1737 Buried at Blackley Jan 1793

Wm Bapt at Blackley Dec 3 1724 Married at Manchester Dec 6 1746 Buried at Blackley Feb 27 1804

John Bapt at Blackley Dec 25 1737 Married at Manchester [illegible] 10 1771 Buried at Blackley Feb 3 1803

Wm Bapt at Blackley [illegible] Married at Manchester [illegible] Buried at Blackley

Richard now Living at Blackley

Edmund now Living in London

James Davenport Son of Wm the Elder

Samuel and Wm Sons of [illegible]

Supposed pedigree from Sir William Davenport to Richard, probably written by George Webster (*Chetham's Library*)

advice, and at one point it even seemed that his claim might be taken further, being considered by his advisers as superior to Edmund's, but in spite of Richard's hopes his case was labelled 'Difficult and complecated' and it must have been dropped.

A few years later Will Davenport became more positively interested in Edmund's claim, and he was nearly persuaded to go into the case jointly with him. This did not materialise, and Will may for a time have been interested in the claim on his own account. He collected letters up to July 1846 in date, but the number of letters in the later years diminished considerably. Then he either lost interest or was persuaded by the more realistic outlook of his wife and family to drop the case. The letters, in a rough pile, were left in an upstairs room in Rob Andrew's farmhouse. About 1850 Rob Andrew removed and the letters lay forgotten.

The farmhouse was let to Robert Stansfield, a widower with five children, and three generations of the Stansfield family lived in the house before the third Robert Stansfield bought it about 1920. By the beginning of the twentieth century the village of Woodhouses had grown a little and was completely hemmed in by the factory towns, but it was still essentially rural in character. Overlooking Medlock Vale stood the little group of buildings once known as 'Andrew's Fold', now called 'Stansfield Fold', and the grocery and all-sorts shop kept by the ladies of the Stansfield family provided a special treat for the children of the village with its superb ginger-beer!

When the house became his own the third Robert Stansfield decided to make the room above the shop, hitherto used for storage, into a bedroom. His wife, therefore, proceeded to turn out the débris of several generations, and in doing so she found the old letters, loosely folded in dusty paper. They had, of course, no connection with the Stansfield family as such. They were hard to decipher and many were difficult or impossible to comprehend, but even on a superficial reading the sad picture of Edmund Davenport emerged so vividly that they were saved from destruction by the family into whose hands they had fallen.

The letters passed into the possession of the fourth Robert Stansfield and his sister Agnes, who went to live in Alderley Edge. In 1977 they learnt of my special interest in Bramhall and its Hall on the publication of my history (wherein was a very short statement of the disputed inheritance), and they offered the papers to me. The letters were no longer in the order in which they were found: some were torn, others very faded, and parts of some were so ingrained with dust as to be illegible. My first task was to decipher them and to date them, in so far as this was possible. Letters of the 1830s, each consisting of a single sheet of paper folded two or three times, were usually addressed and postmarked (if sent through the official mail) on the outside, and many showed signs of sealing. Envelopes, and postage stamps, were introduced in the 1840s, but no envelopes were kept for any of the later letters, so valuable clues were often missing.

I found the collection to be a miscellaneous one of about eighty items; letters written by different people to different people, undated notes and memoranda. The claim of the Davenport family of Blackley to the property in Bramhall was the unifying theme. It was not long before I realised that Will Davenport was the man on the spot who had both the interest and the opportunity to obtain the letters (two of which were actually addressed to him), and in my reconstuction I have credited him with the responsibility for their collection. Robert Andrew stored them for him. They were found in Robert Andrew's farmhouse, and their dates in the 1830s and 1840s coincide with the time he was actually living there. One of the letters is addressed to him, and another (which I have already quoted) mentions him by name. The story of the little coterie at Dyson's, as I have outlined it above, began to unfold itself, but it was a story without beginning and without end. The letters gave me a picture of Will Davenport and his friends avidly collecting every shred of evidence they could lay hands on concerning Will's family's claim, but they did not tell me how Will used this evidence; they could not fully tell me Will's story. Even less could they tell me the story of his cousin Richard, that shadowy yet pathetic figure representative of a whole class of workers whose means of subsistence had been taken from them by the inventions of the new industrial age.

The *Woodhouses Letters* did tell me a great deal about Will's cousin Edmund, who commenced a lawsuit and was imprisoned for the costs. Very personal letters from Edmund –

letters which he would never dream that any twentieth-century eye would scan – reveal him as an honest man with an overriding purpose in life, not as an impostor who saw a chance of becoming rich at some-one else's expense. Edmund was probably mistaken in his claim and certainly obsessed by it, but because he believed so whole-heartedly in his cause he prosecuted it to the utmost extent that the law permitted. Did he have justice done? Other records of Edmund Davenport's case remain and they open up an exciting piece of research. The picture evoked by 'The Meeting Time' fades away, and the figure of Edmund Davenport emerges.

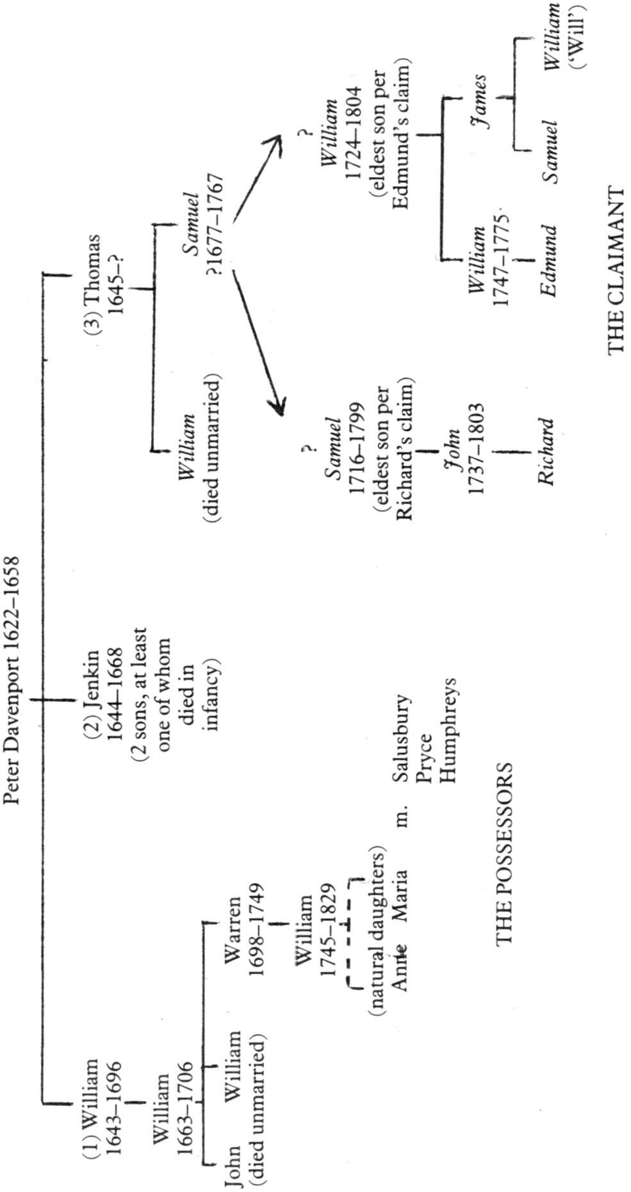

Table of descent of Davenport of Bramhall, showing also the claimed collateral line through Thomas, third son of Peter.

II
IMPRISONMENT FOR DEBT: the case of Edmund Davenport (1)

'But if on the Contrary as the Plaintiff has good reason to believe the Late William Davenport in addition to his Manor and Manor House Did Purches sundre other Estates or Parcels of Property which Latter he gave to his Daughter or his Daughter's Husband Leaving the Bramhall Estate to go to the Davenports which was the Constant Practice with the old Cheshire families who were Proud and justly Proud of Trancemitting their family Estates in long Lines of Ancestry from Generation to Generation then will the Plaintiff's Title to the Property in question be Clear and indisputable'.

From 'The opening speech of Mr Temple the leading Councel for the Plaintiff Edmund Davenport'
as copied by George Webster and put with the *Woodhouses Letters*

'If I could find frinds to Rice to assist me again I would sacrifice 3 parts out of 4 to see wether I have had Justice done me Now or Not'.

Edmund Davenport to Robert Whittam
c27 October 1835

Edmund Davenport was a very ordinary man and would be entirely forgotten now were it not that he dared to lay claim to a valuable estate some two to three miles south of Stockport. Edmund was not in any way unique; there were many similar cases involving so-called heirs at law in the nineteenth century, for the value placed on land was so great, and the theory of primogeniture (succession through the eldest son or the nearest male relative of the full blood) still held sway. By pressing his claim Edmund managed to make himself in some small way notorious, but he also destroyed for himself all semblance of a comfortable life.

Perhaps his life would have been one of penury and misery in any case for he was born a member of the 'inferior classes'. He was baptised in Blackley, Lancashire, on Christmas Day 1771, the son of a weaver. Blackley (pronounced 'Blakeley') was then a hamlet some two miles north of Manchester. It was a wild and desolate region, the people noted for their hardiness and rugged character. An earlier Davenport of Blackley (probably a great-uncle of Edmund and the grandfather of Richard) showed this side of the Blackley character in 1763 when he was sexton of the episcopal chapel.[1] A new incumbent was to be appointed, nominated by the warden and fellows of the collegiate church of Manchester. The parishioners of Blackley had another man in mind. They ordered their sexton, Samuel Davenport, to lock the church against the Manchester nominee and to keep it locked. This he did, and nothing could persuade him to allow the new curate-in-charge into the church. Deadlock ensued, until finally a case was brought at the Chester consistory court, Samuel being made a scapegoat for the churchwardens and parishioners of Blackley. He was found guilty of 'contumacious' conduct and excommunicated but in due course the whole agitation fell through. Samuel died an old man in 1799 and was buried in his own churchyard. Samuel's father, the first Davenport to settle in Blackley, had been the village blacksmith, but by the beginning of the nineteenth century all the Davenports of Blackley were weavers. It was the obvious occupation for men and women of humble origin in the cotton district. But were the Davenports really of humble origin? Edmund and other members of the family claimed that they were not. There was a tradition in the family that their origins were to be found in an ancient and respected family of Cheshire landowners, the Davenports of Bramhall. This, if true, would mean that there had been a very big drop in status from that of gentleman to that of handloom weaver, but such a drop was not impossible, especially when descent was claimed from a younger son. The tradition, however, was never proved.

Edmund's father died when the boy was about four years old. There was a younger brother, Noah, and in due course both brothers enlisted in the army. Noah was killed at Waterloo. Edmund served in the 22nd Light Dragoons from 1794 until the disbanding of the regiment in 1802. He was first sent to Ireland, where British troops were used to quell the rising of

1798, and he was wounded at Antrim, in the same charge as his commander, Colonel Lumley. In 1801 Edmund's regiment joined the British expedition to Egypt, sent to clear out the French forces left in that country by Napoleon. He served throughout the campaign, which was completely successful, but here he contracted ophthalmia, a disease of the eye the effects of which remained with him for many years afterwards. For approximately another eleven years Edmund served as a volunteer in Ireland. At some time he married and had a family, though there were probably no sons to succeed him. In later life he seems to have felt nearest to his uncle James, his father's brother. When the last William Davenport of Bramhall died in 1829 and the legitimate line came to an end Edmund was living in London. He had no pension from the army, and twenty years later he was still described as 'in the Manchester trade' though he had not lived in Manchester for years.

William Davenport Esq., of Bramall Hall in north east Cheshire, was the representative of the fourteenth generation of an unbroken line of Davenports who had been lords of the manor of Bramhall[2] since the time of Edward III. William and his wife Martha had no children, but William had (or thought he had) two illegitimate daughters, whom he adopted and brought up at Bramall Hall. Legal adoption was still in the future, and when William Davenport took the two girls into his home he could only offer a sort of unofficial wardship. According to the researches of J. P. Earwaker, Maria, the younger daughter, who became her father's heiress, was born on 10 April 1785. Earwaker calls her 'Maria Brooke, *alias* Davenport', and it was under the surname of 'Brooke' that she was married. The circumstances of her birth (and that of her sister Anne) were the subject of speculation in Bramhall and the neighbouring town of Stockport throughout much of the nineteenth century.[3] The name of their mother appears in jottings and notes of the time as Margaret, Peggy or Peg Brooke, but who she was is not so certain. She may have been the daughter of a Davenport tenant living at Damery Farm, quite near to Bramall Hall. If so, she was a woman of doubtful reputation, for this 'Peg Brooks' was said to have had five children all by different men, and there was a rumour in Bramhall that on her deathbed Peg confessed that neither Anne

Bramall Hall: east front in the days of the Davenports (*Metropolitan Borough of Stockport*)

nor Maria was by William Davenport. Alternatively, she may have been a 'Peggy Brooke' who at some time lived in the old cruik cottage which, after the coming of the railway, became the home of the Bramhall stationmaster. The truth of these stories cannot be ascertained, but they give force to the claims of other branches of the Davenport family that the Bramhall estate should not be allowed to pass out of the hands of the legitimate line.

In due course both girls married. Anne made a mésalliance, according to the standards of the day, marrying her father's coachman against William Davenport's wishes, but Maria made a 'good' marriage, becoming the wife of Salusbury Pryce Humphreys, a captain in the Royal Navy. Humphreys, too, had a past to live down, though of a very different nature from that of his prospective wife. He had entered the navy as a midshipman in 1790, when he was barely twelve years old, and he very soon gained promotion, proving himself an intrepid seaman who might have expected a great future in the navy. The *Chesapeake* and *Leopard* incident in 1807, when Humphreys had fired on and forcibly boarded the American frigate *Chesapeake* in order to take off British deserters, brought his career to a sudden end. He was recalled by the Admiralty in an effort to placate the infuriated United States and, although he had acted on the positive order of his superior officer, Vice-Admiral Berkeley, he was never offered another naval command. Three years afterwards Humphreys married Maria Brooke of Bramall Hall at Stockport Parish Church. He was then a widower with one young son and, according to Edmund Davenport, he was, or had been, William Davenport's steward. At first he still hoped for a career in the navy, but even after the *Chesapeake* was taken a second time by the British following the famous 'ocean duel' with the *Shannon*, his earnest request for a renewed command was disregarded. It is not surprising if Humphreys now saw his career opening out in another direction, that of country gentleman and lord of the manor of Bramhall. He settled down at Bramall Hall and became a magistrate for Cheshire and a deputy lieutenant for that county. When William Davenport, his father-in-law, died in 1829, Salusbury Pryce Humphreys slipped quietly into the position which had been vacated.

William Davenport of Bramhall (1745–1829) (*Metropolitan Borough of Stockport* and *Sir David Davenport–Handley*)

It was hardly likely, however, that he would be allowed unchallenged possession. The rule of primogeniture (descent to the eldest son to the exclusion of all others, or, on the failure of issue, to the eldest male relative of the senior line) had long been accepted as the proper method of deciding the inheritance of estates; it was a rule recognised by law when anyone possessed of real property (land) died intestate, and strengthened by custom with the tendency of large landowners to entail their estates on their heirs male. (Once an estate was entailed, successive heirs could not dispose of it by will or by deed and it descended automatically from male heir to male heir unless some way could be found to break the entail.) There were Davenports in other parts of the country who claimed relationship with the Bramhall family, but their relationship was distant and not easy of proof for there were now no living descendants of the last two generations of Davenport of Bramhall. The nearest common ancestor was said to be Peter Davenport of Commonwealth times, the great-great-grandfather of the last William. Peter died in 1658 leaving several young children, and it was through his third son Thomas that nineteenth century Davenports (including Edmund) claimed descent.

There was, and still remains, a mystery concerning this Thomas Davenport. Did he ever grow to manhood, or did he die young? His baptism is recorded in the Stockport register on 8 November 1645, but nothing more. There is no record either there or elsewhere of his marriage or his burial; no record, that is, that can with certainty be taken to refer to Thomas of Bramhall. Yet in the nineteenth century at least one other branch of the Davenport family, living far distant from the Blackley Davenports, claimed descent from Thomas.[4] This is a strange mistake if Thomas did indeed die young. Peter Davenport left other sons (exclusive of his eldest son William through whom the line was maintained) who grew up and married. How much more likely that they should have descendants! The Davenports of Blackley claimed that about 1663 Thomas married a daughter of the Davenport family of Wheltrough, near Macclesfield (a branch of the family that was fast sinking into penury), but this was a marriage they never proved. Thomas's eldest surviving son, so they said, was the

Samuel Davenport who became the blacksmith of Blackley. Both Richard and Edmund were his great-grandchildren. Richard, as we have seen, was desperate for the help that just a little of the wealth of the Bramhall estate could have given him; Edmund became obsessed with the idea that Bramhall was his birthright. This estate of near three thousand acres – an estate of small farms and tenant farmers – was as yet untouched by the Industrial Revolution which had brought such change to Stockport, Manchester and the surrounding towns. It embodied the long-held British belief that wealth and power were based on land. It offered Edmund everything he had not got. He had been to Bramhall with his cousin Will and seen at least the outside of the Davenport ancestral home, timber-framed and massive, most of it reconstructed in the time of the first Elizabeth, other parts going back to the fourteenth century. He had met the butler, William Orme. He had tried to make contact with William Davenport, but had been repulsed (so he said) by Captain Humphreys, 'the old man being entirely under the controul of his steward'.[5] Before William Davenport died Edmund was making plans to contest the Bramhall estate.

* * *

In order to be successful in his claim Edmund had firstly to prove his descent from Peter Davenport, demonstrating that he was the eldest living male in the eldest line of that descent. Secondly, he must either be able to cite some old deed of settlement which entailed the estate (depriving William Davenport of the power to give it away) and which made him the next lawful owner after William Davenport, or he must show that William Davenport died intestate thus making him, Edmund, the heir at law according to the rules of primogeniture. Edmund fully appreciated the necessity of proving his descent with accuracy (even if he did not succeed in doing so), but it is doubtful whether he really understood the other alternatives. The *Woodhouses Letters* show that he was convinced William Davenport could not give the estate away, but the legal basis of this belief was a matter to be decided by his advisers.

William Davenport of Bramhall, last of his line, died on 14 April 1829, and three weeks later Edmund Davenport laid formal claim to the property by serving notices on Captain Humphreys and the thirty or so tenants on the estate. He claimed as 'heir at law and oldest male descendant of the surviving male branch of the family of Davenport' and demanded 'the quiet and peaceable possession' of the Bramhall estate and the payment of rents 'unto me my agent or Solicitor', otherwise he threatened action; he would 'institute such proceedings . . . as my counsel or attorney shall advise'. At the same time Edmund's solicitors commenced a search for William Davenport's will and for the various certificates necessary to establish their client's pedigree. Wills were not publicly available as now, and watch had to be kept at the diocesan registry at Chester. The will was proved by Salusbury Pryce Humphreys before the rector of Stockport, acting as surrogate, on 8 August 1829, but whether Edmund ever saw a copy is not certain. The question becomes significant in the later conduct of his case.

Several times during the next eighteen months Edmund Davenport required, through his lawyers, possession of the Bramhall estate. This was denied him. Captain Humphreys was in possession, and the only way in which he could be legally dispossessed was by bringing an action of ejectment against him. This was an action which must be brought in a court of common law, but before he could consider bringing it with any real chance of success Edmund needed to know by what authority, if any, Salusbury Pryce Humphreys held the estate. Captain Humphreys and his wife do appear to have told him that deeds in their favour had been executed by William Davenport shortly before his death, but they refused Edmund perusal of these deeds. At that time it was beyond the power of a court of common law to order the production or 'discovery' of a document which one of the parties did not choose to show to his opponent. Only the Court of Chancery (a court of 'equity' or 'conscience') could do this, and it was to the Court of Chancery that Edmund had to apply for production of proofs of title. In 1831 he filed his Bill of Discovery, thereby commencing the case, and incurring the costs, which were to be his undoing.

In his bill (a lengthy document as all such bills were) Edmund claimed descent from Peter Davenport of Bramhall whose father, so he said, had created certain trusts which entailed the

Bramhall lands on the heirs male of the Davenport family for a very long term of years. The type of entail described – intended to keep property within the same family for as long a period as possible – was frequently made in the Commonwealth period when landowners were especially anxious to guard their estates against political plundering. English law, however, was never happy with these attempts to create 'perpetuities', and whether the courts would, in the nineteenth century, have admitted the validity of a settlement which took the inheritance through six generations is dubious. The trust deeds, if they ever existed, would have had to be kept throughout these years in a muniments room at Bramall Hall, for bank strong rooms were unknown. Captain Humphreys denied that he had any such deeds, and there is no reason to disbelieve him, though neither is there any clue as to what, if anything, had been their fate.

A Chancery bill of this period contained a long list of 'interrogatories' which the defendants were required to answer on oath. Oral evidence was not permitted in the Court of Chancery; each witness was secretly examined by specially appointed commissioners sent into the country, and written depositions were returned to the court. Captain Humphreys denied that he had any knowledge of matters bearing on Edmund Davenport's petition, and he entered a demurrer; that is, he objected to the bill on a point of law. He denied that Edmund Davenport had any right to be given 'discovery'. The demurrer was considered on 25 July 1831 by Sir Lancelot Shadwell, the Vice-Chancellor of England, and it was 'held to be good' and allowed. Discovery of documents was only permitted in cases where those documents would help the case of the plaintiff, and not when their sole use would be for the defence. This is the probable reason why Edmund Davenport failed on the demurrer. For the time being he could go no further and, worse than that, he now found himself in debt to Captain Humphreys for the costs both of the bill and the demurrer, a total amount of £65 12s 1d.

Edmund Davenport did not pay the costs – he could not pay them – and for a time Salusbury Pryce Humphreys did not try to exact the money from him. Instead of giving up the case, however, Edmund made preparations to proceed in a different way; he applied for a court order to prosecute his suit *in forma pauperis*. This method of procedure, which dated back to the time of Henry VIII, can be considered as a very inferior substitute for our modern system of legal aid, but because of its inherent disadvantages it was comparatively little used by the beginning of the nineteenth century. The procedure was entirely under the control of the courts and by it poor persons could obtain free the writs necessary for commencing an action and the services of counsel and solicitors. There was no legal aid fund out of which counsel or solicitor could be paid, and lawyers nominated by the courts, who must give their services free, could hardly have regarded *in forma pauperis* cases with great enthusiasm. Further, the courts found difficulty in sorting out the genuine from the 'vexatious' applicants, and in an attempt to solve this problem, which was really an administrative one, they would ask to be assured of the merits of the case, thus creating a vicious circle for the applicant who could not afford a preliminary brief to counsel, but not necessarily deterring the fraudulent. How Edmund Davenport overcame this difficulty we do not know; perhaps the fact that he had already brought a reasonable-looking case may have helped. In order to qualify as a 'poor person' he had also to make declaration on oath that he was not worth more than £5 in the world, apart from the clothes he stood up in. This he must have done, and in January 1832 he obtained his *in forma pauperis* order.

The following month he put in his appeal against the order allowing the demurrer. He then returned to Manchester for a time – perhaps he visited Bramhall – but towards the end of March he had to leave Manchester hurriedly as friends warned him that 'certain parties' intended to put him into a private madhouse. This danger was not to be ignored in the conditions of the mid-nineteenth century, whether or not the information was correct. Little was known of mental illness at that time, and certification of insanity by any two medical men was sufficient to incarcerate both genuine and not-so-genuine cases in a privately-run lunatic asylum for quite a long time.

Old James Davenport, father of Will and uncle to Edmund, was not happy about the way things were going. He must have felt degraded at Edmund's acceptance of the status of a pauper, but Edmund wrote to him from London to reassure him. 'You accuse me of having injured you', said Edmund, 'but should I be successful neither you nor Richard Davenport [his rival cousin, not one of uncle James's sons] nor any of my relations will I forget, but you will most assuredly participate in my good fortune – therefore for the present you had better remain quiet and anything that occurs particular I shall send you word'. Edmund was looking for new friends, and thought he had found someone who would furnish money so that the case would not be brought 'under the paupers act'.[6]

Nothing happened for a while. The Court of Chancery was notoriously slow and Edmund Davenport's appeal was not immediately heard. Edmund remained in London, and obtained news of events in Bramhall from friends. In the summer of 1832 Captain Humphreys threatened Lomas (a tenant who was friendly towards Edmund Davenport) with ejectment, and there was a dispute about the possession of some common land. As the lord of the manor claimed legal jurisdiction over the 'common' or 'waste' in his manor, this was a vital question for Edmund Davenport. 'Under no pretence whatever are you to give Possession of it to any one but me', wrote Edmund of this particular piece of land. Timber, too, was important, for it represented part of the wealth of the estate, and Edmund was anxious to know whether Captain Humphreys felled any trees. Although his Stockport friends (who saw things from a different point of view) seemed downhearted, Edmund himself continued to be optimistic concerning the result of his case.

His appeal was heard by the Lord Chancellor, Lord Brougham, on 10 December 1833. Brougham became Chancellor when the Whigs came to power in 1830, and he found a very long list of Chancery cases waiting to be dealt with. The delays and abuses of the Chancery had become a national disgrace. Brougham, with all a reformer's zeal, was determined to clear up the mess, and he worked long and hard to do so, but he underrated the difficulty of the task and, in consequence, his judgments were sometimes hurried and superficial. We wonder how much care he took over this particular case, a case which was of little significance to any but the plaintiff and the defendant, and which did not merit any report.

Brougham dismissed Edmund Davenport's appeal without

costs. Years later Edmund told a friend that the Lord Chancellor had said there was not a link in his pedigree wanting; unquestionably he was the heir at law. It is difficult for us to assess this statement. Proof of identity of the various people through whom Edmund claimed descent would have to be given at the hearing. Here is a summary of his claim, as given in the bill of discovery.

Thomas (3rd son of Peter Davenport of Bramhall)

- William, died without issue
- Samuel d 1767
  - William d 1804
    - William d 1775
      - Edmund

Edmund ignored the second Samuel Davenport of Blackley (Richard's grandfather) in his pedigree, claiming that William, his own grandfather, was the eldest son of the first Samuel. However, it was not through any dispute over the marriage of Samuel, nor yet over the identity of Thomas, his supposed father, that Edmund's case was upset. Whatever the views of the Lord Chancellor upon his pedigree, Edmund failed, so he himself admitted, through a technical fault in his bill.

* * *

At the end of the year 1833 Edmund had to face the fact that he had failed completely in Chancery. Salusbury Pryce Humphreys was secure in his possession, and, we may be sure, was collecting the rents and managing the estate as efficiently as any Davenport. On 21 February 1834 he was knighted by William IV, the sailor king, and from henceforth gained in status and must be called 'Sir Salusbury'. Nevertheless Edmund did not give up. He was pursuing other methods of pressing his case, and he had found two friends to constitute themselves as his agents.

First there was Thomas Sharpe, a pottery manufacturer of Swadlincote in south Derbyshire. Sharpe had set up his own

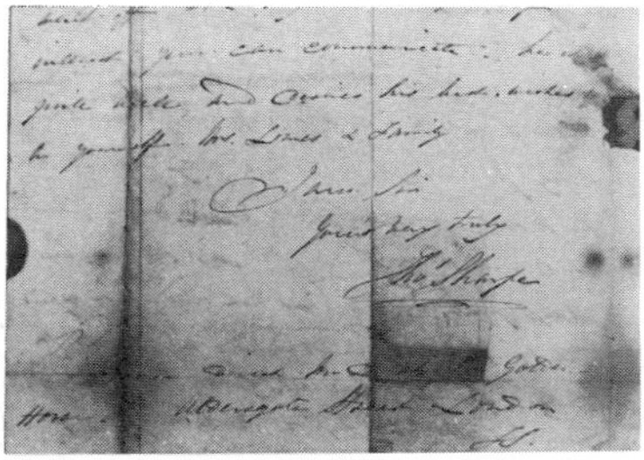

Top: Sharpe Brothers Industrial Estate: the setting today (*E. B. Dean*); *Bottom Left:* Shell of the last remaining kiln on Thomas Sharpe's pottery works (*T. B. Dean*); *Bottom Right:* Signature of Thomas Sharpe (*Chetham's Library*)

business in 1821 in what was then only a small hamlet, but by 1834 he had become a man of means and influence in this rapidly expanding district of coal mines and pottery kilns. He espoused Edmund Davenport's cause (for what reason we do not know) and provided money. Peter Morrison, Edmund's other friend, acted as Sharpe's second-in-command and business manager. Morrison lived at No. 1, Bartholomew Lane, in the city of London just opposite to the Bank of England. This site housed, and still houses, the offices of the Alliance Assurance Company (now the Sun Alliance), and possibly Morrison was a resident employee of that company. He wrote a large, flowing hand, and could pen a typical business letter.

Even though he had failed in Chancery it was still possible for Edmund Davenport (if he thought it worth while) to try his action of ejectment at common law, and this, with Thomas Sharpe's help, he now prepared to do. The Declaration in Ejectment – the notice required to commence the action – was served on Sir Salusbury Pryce Humphreys towards the end of 1834 and the case was heard the following August. Meanwhile Thomas Sharpe attempted to make an 'entry' on the Bramhall estate in the name of Edmund Davenport, and during most of the year 1834 and part of 1835 he was trying various ways of achieving this end. All his efforts ended in failure, and he was forced to recognise that the ejectment trial was the only way in which Sir Salusbury could possibly be dispossessed.

Early in 1834 we find Thomas Sharpe looking for a man on the spot through whom Edmund's business in Bramhall could be conducted. He met, and made arrangements with, Hugh Knowles, the owner of two or three cottages (in one of which he lived) and of the *Anchor* inn in 'Bullock Smithy', the present Hazel Grove. Knowles, who owed no allegiance to Sir Salusbury Pryce Humphreys, was a man of independent means and of some small importance in his own district, and his *Anchor* inn, just outside the eastern boundary of the Bramhall estate, offered a convenient centre for the various people coming from London on Edmund's business. During March Peter Morrison accompanied Edmund Davenport to Bullock Smithy, and they served notices on the Bramhall tenants restating Edmund's claim and offering a guarantee to such tenants as would pay rent to him. The notices had little effect, and once more Edmund Davenport was obliged to return to London in a hurry, 'hunted', said Morrison, 'from his *Home* and kind friends with so little ceremony or time'.[7] Peter Morrison stayed in the district a little longer, returning to London at the beginning of April. He had found a case which he thought he could follow up on Edmund's behalf, and his subsequent correspondence with Hugh Knowles illustrates the practice, common at the time, of sending long distance letters by the guard of a stage coach if possible. This could be a cheaper way than paying the official postage which was then charged according to distance. Morrison asked for a reply by 'Bailey guard of the Peverill' when that coach next passed through Bullock Smithy on its way from Manchester to London. No doubt Morrison had already travelled by that ever-popular coach 'Peveril of the Peak' and knew the guard well. But his plans came to nothing.

Thomas Sharpe obviously still hoped that he could induce the Bramhall tenants to pay their rent to Edmund Davenport, or, at the least, to withhold the money from Salusbury Pryce Humphreys, and to this end he intended that either he or Morrison should be in Bramhall when the next rent day came round. In the event neither was present, and no doubt the rents were collected as usual for Salusbury Pryce Humphreys. However, Edmund's friends in London were still confident, and Thomas Sharpe wrote to a friendly Bramhall tenant that 'the Squire's case [by which he meant the ejectment case] is now proceeding with every probability of speedy success'.[8]

In the autumn of 1834 Sharpe and Morrison took a new step. They sent two men from London to Bramhall to try to induce the Bramhall tenants – or some of them – to attorn to Edmund Davenport. These men were sent to the *Anchor* inn with money and a letter of introduction from Morrison requesting Hugh Knowles to help them 'in forwarding the object they have in view'. One of them, John Ham, made a great friend of Knowles during his stay in Bramhall, and on his return to London he wrote long letters which Knowles eventually passed over to Will Davenport of Woodhouses. The other man, whom we only know by his surname, 'Chase', was more solitary and kept himself aloof from the others. Ham and Chase received their instructions from Peter Morrison in London, and the whole business was conducted through his firm of London solicitors, Messrs Johnson & Wetherall. The formal recognition of Edmund Davenport as lord of the manor, which they sought, was to be ratified by the payment of one shilling on the part of every tenant attorning, while Edmund Davenport, on his side, undertook that the tenant would not be distrained on for rent.

It was not to be expected that Sir Salusbury Pryce Humphreys would relish these proceedings. Edmund Davenport still had not paid the costs of the Chancery suit, and it was within Sir Salusbury's legal rights to have Edmund imprisoned for debt. He had already obtained the taxed (i.e. officially certified) certificates of costs, and he instructed his solicitor, John Kenyon Winterbottom, to apply for attachments against Edmund Davenport. (A writ of attachment ordered the sheriff of the county concerned to arrest and detain the debtor until his debts had been duly settled.) In the first week of November 1834 warrants for Edmund's arrest were issued. His period of freedom was rapidly coming to an end.

Meanwhile Ham and Chase continued their work with the Bramhall tenantry. John Ham was officiously busy and outwardly successful (in his own estimation), but we can see him as essentially a timid and unadventurous character. Chase, of whom we only have second-hand knowledge, must have been a very different type of person. He was efficient even to the extent of exceeding instructions, for in the second week in November it appeared that he had made a seizure. Who the unfortunate tenant might be whose goods Chase seized in lieu of rent we do not know, but Johnson & Wetherall, the solicitors, immediately sent instructions that he was to stop any further proceedings on behalf of Edmund Davenport. John Ham, shocked and fearful, at once stopped his proceedings, too, and left Bullock Smithy leaving his bill unpaid. He made for Swadlincote to report to Thomas Sharpe. On the afternoon of Friday 21 November 1834 he reached Derby. (He later wrote to Knowles that he 'found all right except my old Shoes'. Did he walk all the way?) On Saturday morning he walked sixteen miles to Ashby-de-la-Zouch and then the remaining seven miles to Swadlincote, 'and never tasted bit or drop by the way'. Fortunately his reception by Thomas Sharpe was friendly and he stayed until Tuesday, Sharpe then driving him back in his carriage to Derby so that he could continue his journey to Nottingham and London. During the weekend John Ham saw something of the pottery works of his host. 'He is a Gentn of large property & his potteries are like a little Town', wrote Ham to Knowles, describing both Sharpe and his business in one graphic sentence.[9]

Edmund Davenport was not unduly worried about Chase's seizure. His solicitor had told him he could make a seizure every rent day if he so desired, 'and that', declared Edmund, 'I sertenley will and I hope I shall make A Better Job than as been made this time'. However he was getting very uneasy because he had neither seen nor heard anything of his two Bramhall agents for some time. Knowles had written with depressing news from Bullock Smithy. ('You said in your Letter that Mr Chase was Actining very Ronge which I am sorrey to hear', wrote Edmund in reply.[10]) When exact news came, matters were even worse than Edmund anticipated. Chase was accused of illegally taking money from Bramhall tenants, and particularly from a widow, Mrs Thorpe, who might not have the knowledge or the will to refuse his demands. Edmund had to write to Widow Thorpe asking whether she had indeed paid Chase and, if so, in whose name he had given her a receipt.

Not all Edmund Davenport's friends blamed Chase for the failure of his affairs in Bramhall. James Hulme, an earthenware dealer in Stockport, who comes into the story later as the man who did most for Edmund Davenport's cause in Bramhall, regarded Ham with a suspicious eye. He even went so far as to write individually to Edmund Davenport, Thomas Sharpe and Peter Morrison, warning them that Ham had become dangerously intimate with John Cooke, the Bramhall steward, as well as with others on the estate, and that now that he was back in London he was carrying on a very private correspondence with Hugh Knowles of Bullock Smithy. Hulme's letters caused more consternation in Edmund Davenport's little circle in London, but Ham managed to vindicate himself. John Ham looked upon everything that had occurred as a plot, deeply laid by Chase against himself. Meanwhile Chase had not appeared in London to answer for his own actions, even though money had been sent to enable him to return.

At the end of November Sir Salusbury Pryce Humphreys put in his reply to the declaration in ejectment. Edmund Davenport called it 'Nothing only what is comnley put in with Every Ejectment';[11] in other words Sir Salusbury had pleaded the 'general issue', denying Edmund's claim completely and giving himself latitude to concentrate his defence on whatever aspect of the case he felt most likely to be successful.

A few days later came Edmund Davenport's arrest. He and his wife were living in Old Street, just north of the City, and for three or four weeks the warrants had been out against him; the sheriff's officers had only to run their quarry to earth in order to take him. Information was laid against Edmund Davenport, and on 3 December 1834 he was arrested by an officer of the sheriff of Middlesex. He spent one night in the sheriff's officer's lock-up and the next day he was taken to Whitecross Street prison in the City of London.

* * *

Edmund Davenport was in Whitecross Street prison for only twelve days. During all or part of that time Thomas Sharpe was in London arranging his affairs and trying to effect an improvement in his situation.

First Sharpe tried to get Edmund Davenport liberated. This could, of course, have been done by paying the costs for which he was imprisoned, but Sharpe never seems to have been prepared to go so far as this. The ejectment trial was expected to come on soon and, if it was successful, matters would settle themselves. Sharpe also had some doubts as to whether the arrest was legal, and the solicitors, Johnson & Wetherall, were instructed to look into the matter and to procure Edmund Davenport's freedom if at all possible. Next, Sharpe had to deal with the tenants from whom money had been illegally taken. This money must be recovered from Chase and repaid, if possible, though Sharpe intended also to cover himself in the matter. Finally there was a bill from the landlord of the *Anchor* awaiting attention.

Johnson & Wetherall's efforts to procure Edmund Davenport's release proved unsuccessful, but so, at the same time, did the efforts of Sir Salusbury's solicitors to put an end to

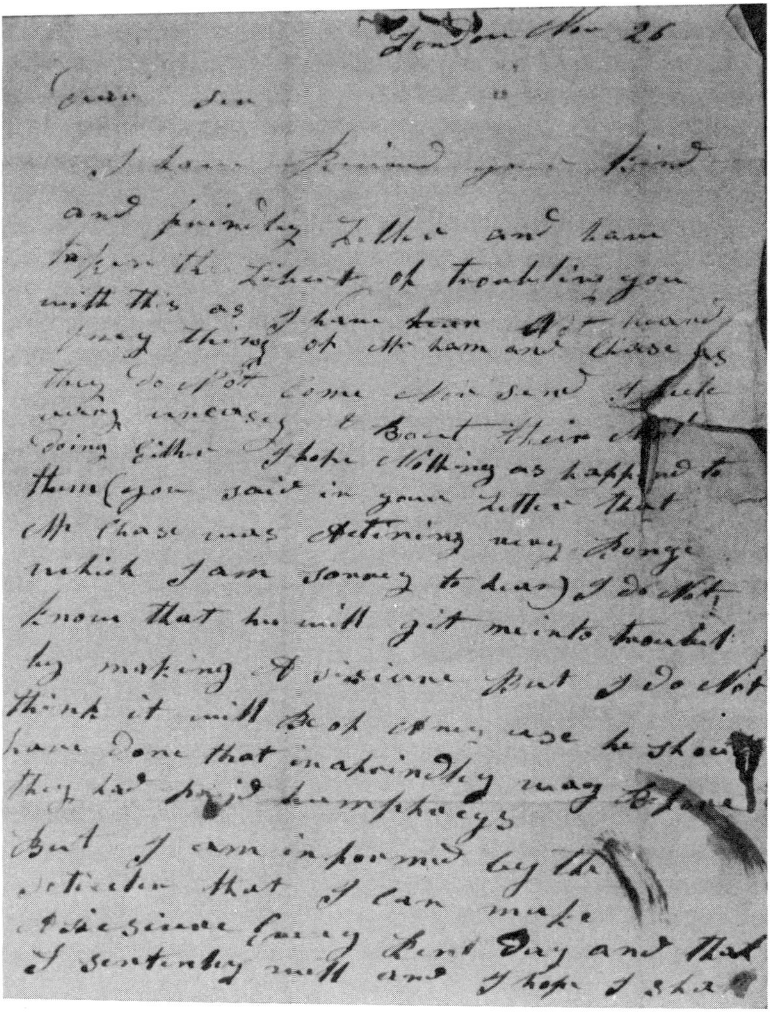

London Nov 26

Dear Sir

I have Recived your kind and friendly Letter and have taken the Liberty of troubling you with this as I have been Not heard any thing of Mr ham and Chase as they do Not come Near send & feele very uneasy about their not doing Either I hope Nothing as happend to them (you said in your Letter that Mr Chase was Detaining very Strange which I am sorrey to hear) I do Not know that he will git me into trouble by making a Desicione But I do Not think it will be of any use he shou[ld] have done that in a friendly way they had paid humphreys Before But I am informed by the detective that I can make Desicione Every Rent Day and that I sertenly will and I hope I sha[ll]

Edmund Davenport to Hugh Knowles, 26 Nov., (1834) (*Chetham's Library*)

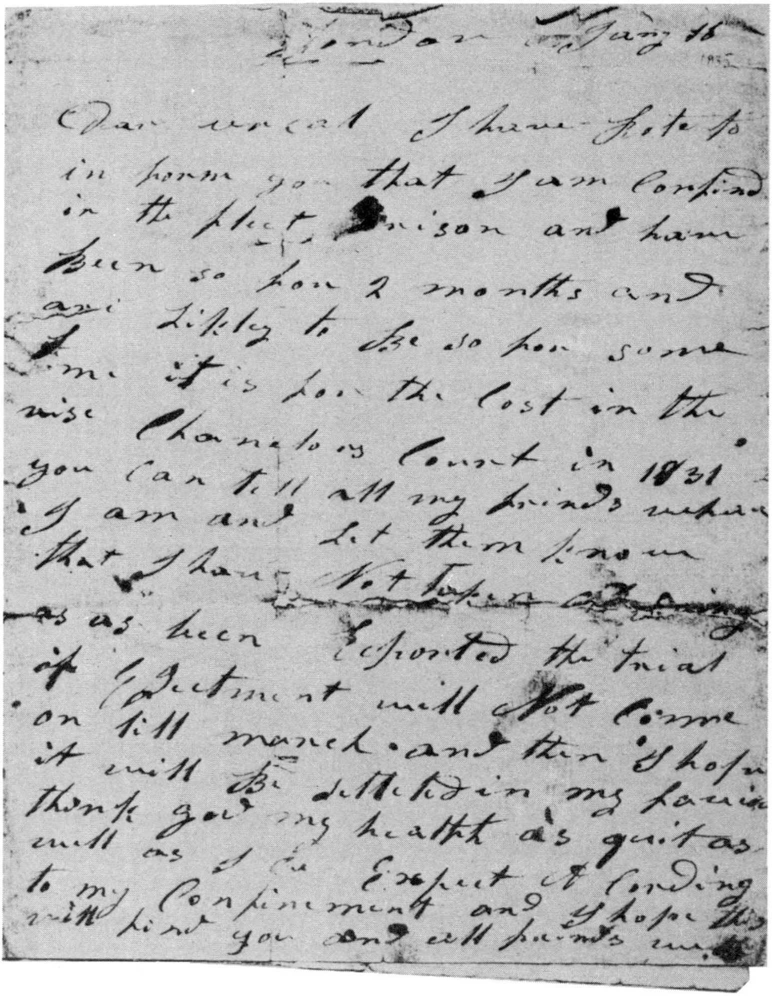
London Jany 16
1835

Dear uncal I have rote to
in form you that I am Confind
in the flet Prison and have
been so for 2 months and
am Likley to Bee so for some
time it is for the Cost in the
wise Chancelory Court in 1831
you can tell all my friends where
I am and Let them know
that I have Not Taken [illegible]
as as been Reported the trial
of Indictment will Not Comme
on till march. and then I hope
it will Be settled in my favour
thank god my health as quite as
well as I Ever Expect it Conding
to my Confinement and I hope this
will find you and all friends we

Edmund Davenport to James Davenport, 16 Jan., 1835 (*Chetham's Library*)

The Fleet Prison, (*Guildhall Library*)

the case altogether. Lord Lyndhurst had now succeeded Brougham as lord chancellor, and Winterbottom, the solicitor, applied to him for an injunction forbidding Edmund Davenport to proceed further with his suit. This was refused, Lord Lyndhurst observing (according to Ham) that 'it was quite enough for the Man to be imprisoned for the Costs of the suit & therefore he was bound to allow him to try his question of Right!!!'[12] (The three exclamation marks seem typical of John Ham.) Edmund Davenport could still proceed with his case (in so far as he was able) from prison.

Before he left London Thomas Sharpe took out a writ to remove Edmund Davenport from Whitecross Street to the Fleet Prison. In the Fleet (as in all the London prisons) there was much squalor, but there might also be comfort of a sort; in Whitecross Street prison there was no comfort. In mid-December 1834 Edmund Davenport was lodged in the Fleet, and on 16 January 1835 he wrote to his uncle, James Davenport of Middleton, to acquaint him with the position.

> Dear Uncal [Edmund's letter commenced]
> I have Rote to inform you that I am Confind in the fleet prison and have Been so for 2 months and are Likly to Be so for some time it is for the Cost in the vise Chanclors Court in 1831 you can tell all my frinds whire I am . . .

The Fleet Prison – notorious in earlier times as a place of incarceration for those committing offences against the state – had by the nineteenth century become a prison for debtors and persons committed for contempt of the courts of Chancery, Exchequer and Common Pleas. It stood on the east side of Farringdon Street and was a gaunt, brick building, four storeys high, with an exercise area at the back enclosed by high walls. Inside, a gallery lit by a small window at each end ran the length of each storey, and the rooms for the prisoners opened off. These rooms were on the 'Master's side' and must be paid for. It was a tragic farce that those who had money to pay, and might have made some attempt to reduce their debts, were allowed comforts and privileges in prison, while the genuinely penniless were made to suffer merciless hardship. The turnkeys let out the 'Master's side' rooms on a system of 'chummage', which could give them the equivalent of three or four rents for each single room, and the prison was greatly overcrowded. Charles Dickens has described the system in *The Pickwick Papers.*[13] For the benefit of his readers Dickens sent his hero on a tour of the Fleet Prison, and Mr Pickwick spent two nights in the company of some very undesirable personages before he obtained a room to himself. He saw the plight also of prisoners on the 'Poor side', who lived herded together in wretched conditions, but he realised that dirt and squalor were not confined to the poor side and that bribery and abuse of authority abounded everywhere.

The fictional sojourn of Mr Pickwick in the Fleet Prison must almost have coincided with the real imprisonment of Edmund Davenport, for Dickens was writing of the period about 1830. Mr Pickwick, walking along one of the galleries, peeped into some of the rooms, curious to see their occupants. We could almost believe he saw Edmund Davenport himself; if not the Edmund Davenport of 1835, certainly the Edmund Davenport of 1836 and after. This man was 'poring, by the light of a feeble tallow candle, over a bundle of soiled and tattered papers, yellow with dust and dropping to pieces from age: writing, for the hundredth time, some lengthened statement of his grievances, for the perusal of some great man whose eyes it would never reach, or whose heart it would never touch'. In the early stages of his imprisonment, however, Edmund Davenport was not 'solitary', as was Dickens's imaginary prisoner, for he had his wife living with him. There was no restriction on the movement of wives and families in the Fleet, and the number living in swelled to excess the already-overcrowded prison population. In John Ham's rather pompous phraseology, the Davenports gave up their 'establishment' in Old Street, and Mrs Davenport was then free to devote her whole time to the needs of her husband!

Chase returned home to London some time near the beginning of January 1835. He was not apprehended, although John Ham thought there would be a sheriff's officer waiting for him when he arrived, nor did he visit Edmund Davenport when requested to do so. ('D might be D-d he should do as he liked', Chase was reported to have said.[14]) In due course he quietly disappeared again. He had hatched up a new plan with some of his confederates in London. The probable ringleader was a man called George Watts (alias White), described by Edmund Davenport as a short set man of about thirty seven with a very prominent scar on his upper lip. He was the man who had given Edmund away to Winterbottom, the solicitor, and had thus been responsible for his arrest; Watts had been paid £10 for the information. Now he must have realised the lucrative possibilities that the Bramhall tenants presented to both himself and Chase if only they could get back to Bramhall, so in order to find the money Watts told his wife a cock and bull story about obtaining a job as a waiter in Manchester and needing £15 as a deposit for glass etc. . . . The money was raised from his wife's family, and with it Watts and Chase and Chase's son returned to Bramhall, intent on reaping another harvest for themselves from among the tenantry.

In due course Hugh Knowles spotted Chase and his companions on the Bramhall estate, and he at once reported the matter to Edmund Davenport. Complaints were now coming fast from Bramhall to London, and Edmund had to write letters of appeasement, stressing that Chase was acting entirely contrary to orders. Before the end of January prompt action on the part of Hugh Knowles enabled Chase and Watts to be 'arrested in their infamous career' (Ham's phrase), but there followed a very bleak period for Edmund Davenport in his relations with Bramhall people. John Cooke, the steward, and Winterbottom, the solicitor, were doing all that they could to build up a solid tenantry for Sir Salusbury again. They went round the estate suggesting that Edmund Davenport's friends had been 'shy to support him'. Even the allegiance of Hugh Knowles seemed to be wavering, and John Ham wrote to reassure his friend and to give him one or two titbits of information which might favour Edmund's case.

Ham's most dramatic piece of information concerned a conversation between Rev. Matthew Dunn, an elderly clergyman who for many years had been the resident curate of Cheadle in Cheshire, and Sir Salusbury Pryce Humphreys. The parish of Cheadle extended right to the western borders of the Bramhall estate, and Mr Dunn must have known Sir Salusbury well. He was said to have informed Sir Salusbury that, from the registers in his possession, as well as from his own knowledge, 'our Davenport' (Edmund) was the heir to the Bramhall estate.

At this Sir Salusbury 'turned very pale' (with fear or with anger?) and Mr Dunn advised him not to proceed with the cause. Mr Dunn, being friendly with Mr Neale, a hatter in Stockport, passed on the gist of this conversation to him, and Mr Neale told some gentlemen publicly in London. The news reached Edmund Davenport (albeit in a third-hand version) the same day. Alas for John Ham's hopes! From other records we know that Edmund Davenport, or his advisers, must already have examined the Cheadle parish registers for relevant Davenport entries and found them lacking in information.

By the spring of 1835 Edmund Davenport's affairs in Bramhall seem to have been sorted out, and the result of a case at the Chester assizes put new hope into his advisers. The case was brought by James Hulme, Edmund's friend, and in order to understand how it came about it is necessary to go back a few years. In 1826, during the lifetime of William Davenport, Hulme had enclosed a small portion of the 'waste' on the Bramhall estate, having first obtained William Davenport's permission subject to a rental of 2s 6d per annum. As the amount of the rent was purely nominal, its purpose being merely to preserve the right of William Davenport as lord of the manor, the money was never claimed in his lifetime. After his death Captain Humphreys applied for the arrears, but Hulme refused to pay. Humphreys took tbe case to the so-called 'county court' – the old sheriff's court at Chester – and Hulme was forced to pay 7s 6d, an amount which would cover the rental for the three years up to William Davenport's death. Hulme paid no more, for he recognised Edmund Davenport's title, and in 1834 Sir Salusbury distrained on him for four years' rent at 2s 6d a year. Hulme then brought an action of replevin, a remedy available to him for goods unlawfully seized for rent. By it he could reclaim the goods pending trial of the legality of the distraint, but he must also agree to abide by the findings of the court, whatever these might be. Although Hulme's case was seemingly a trivial action for a very small sum of money, it was in reality a trial of the title of Sir Salusbury Pryce Humphreys to the manor of Bramhall, and this was clearly realised by all parties to the trial. It was a rule of law that a tenant could not dispute his landlord's title and Hulme had already, in some sense, recognised his obligation to the Bramhall estate and to the late William Davenport. The purpose of his action of replevin was to put Sir Salusbury on express proof of his title.

Sir Salusbury's case relied heavily on proof of the proceedings in the sheriff's court. The minute book was produced, but it was of no real help as it only showed the amount of money which Hulme had paid over and not the nature of the action. There was a long trial, of which we have no records of the arguments on either side, and finally a verdict was given for *Hulme*! Although this did not positively establish Edmund Davenport's claim as lord of the manor of Bramhall, it certainly negatived that of Salusbury Pryce Humphreys. Edmund's friends were jubilant. Sir Salusbury had engaged three counsel to defend him, 'one with a silk gown', and he must have spent over £300, and he had lost the case! What would the tenants think now? Yet this was not quite the end of the matter. On the morning after the trial the judge 'discovered his error' (an error which must have had something to do with proof of proceedings in the sheriff's court) and he gave Sir Salusbury's counsel leave to move to have the verdict reversed. This piece of information appeared at the end of a short report in the *Stockport Advertiser*, a paper which would wish to do its best for Sir Salusbury. The ultimate outcome of the case is still a mystery.

Sir Salusbury Pryce Humphreys had been expected to bring a case against Chase and his companions at the same Chester assizes, and Edmund Davenport (from prison) and Peter Morrison had been subpoenaed to give evidence, but in view of the set-back he had sustained in Hulme's case Sir Salusbury could hardly proceed further. We therefore hear no more of this little band of rogues.

Sharpe and Morrison, elated by their apparent success at Chester, decided to arrange another rent day in Bramhall at which they would both be present. This time they could not conceive that the tenants would dispute Edmund Davenport's authority. Notices for the tenants were sent to James Hulme for distribution, and Sharpe decided that he personally would see Joseph Lomas, a tenant friendly to Edmund Davenport, who was being threatened with legal action by Salusbury Pryce Humphreys. Lomas had refused to give up some land which Sir Salusbury claimed as part of the Bramhall estate, and he must be provided with legal aid. Thomas Sharpe intended also, as the accredited agent of Edmund Davenport, to receive formally from Lomas the property which he held.

Once again Sharpe's plans in Bramhall were doomed to failure. John Ham was to accompany him on this errand and they planned to travel to Bullock Smithy on Thursday 30 April 1835 by either the *Bruce* or the *Peveril of the Peak*. They had left their arrangements too late; both coaches were full inside for that day. No doubt John Ham would have been expected to travel outside, had he been going alone, but that would hardly have suited Thomas Sharpe, who was not only a gentleman of means but also had bouts of rheumatic gout. Urgent instructions were sent to Hugh Knowles to *see* Lomas and make exact arrangements with him for Mr Sharpe's visit. Sharpe and Ham then travelled the next day by the new *Bee Hive* coach, arriving in Bullock Smithy on Saturday morning, 2 May. They put up at the *Red Lion* inn, not at the *Anchor*, and the interview with Lomas was to take place immediately on their arrival, as a very first priority. Some time later the same day Sharpe instructed Ham to write a formal note to Hugh Knowles inviting him to breakfast with them the following (Sunday) morning. Doubtless Sharpe then intended to acquaint Knowles with the result of his interview with Lomas, and he would also wish to discuss with him the arrangements for their rent day at the *Anchor* on the Monday. But of neither of these transactions do the *Woodhouses Letters* give any further record!

It is not difficult to conjecture that the rent day went badly for Edmund Davenport and that the visit must have been a humiliating experience for Thomas Sharpe. He took few, if any, rents, and he must have become entangled in argument before he (and Morrison) finally left the district. Then a rumour spread round Bramhall that Sharpe and Morrison had intended to leave without paying. Ham, back in London again, dismissed this 'paltry idea' as just 'another proof of what would be trumped up to serve a rotten cause'.[15] Sir Salusbury held the property by what Ham called 'Mob law'; he had money and 'his Bullies' at command. Knowles was worried about reprisals, but John Ham was quickly sanguine again and thought it very unlikely that Sir Salusbury would take any 'unpleasant steps' against the tenants.

Knowles was right and his fears proved justified. At the end of May Sir Salusbury did commence unpleasant proceedings of some kind or another against some of the tenantry. Sharpe now washed his hands of affairs in Bramhall. It was not Davenport's intention, he said, to go to further trouble in matters of dispute between the parties. The 'straightforward way of proceeding' was to concentrate on the forthcoming ejectment case, and go into court prepared to win. It could not concern anyone but the tenants themselves whether they paid two rents or one; when the matter was decided in Edmund Davenport's favour it could be no consideration with him that the tenants had already paid a rent to Salusbury Pryce Humphreys or anyone else.

This was a strange remark for Thomas Sharpe to make. He should have known that, whatever the outcome of the case, the tenants would not be required to pay their rents twice over. A wrongful possessor could be made to pay to the true owner all the rents he had received during the period of his possession, up to a maximum of six years. The prospect of paying out thousands of pounds in so-called 'mesne profits' could be appalling, and quite sufficient to make anyone like Sir Salusbury fight to the utmost to retain the estate.

Thomas Sharpe was entirely right when he said that the ejectment action was the straightforward way of proceeding. It was the only way of proceeding. 'Possession is eleven points of the law and they say there are but twelve' ran an old proverb, emphasising the fact that in early cases of dispute over land, when documentary proof was not always available, the various legal points which decided ownership nearly always came down in favour of the possessor. Possession became a prima facie mark of ownership and entitled the possessor to legal protection until a stronger title than his own had been made out. No effort to oust Sir Salusbury could meet with any legal success until Edmund Davenport first established in himself an independent and superior title to the property. To prepare a careful and watertight case along these lines was more important than to attempt any further interference with the internal management of the Bramhall property, and it was wise of Thomas Sharpe to realise this. Yet even here he was misled. He wrote to Knowles of 'progress in Discoveries made lately' which were highly beneficial to Edmund's case, though he did not say what these discoveries were. Their worthlessness, alas, very soon became apparent.

Meanwhile Edmund Davenport languished in prison. Preparation of the case went on without him, though Peter Morrison assured him that all was well. Late in June 1835 Edmund wrote to his uncle James, expressing his feelings. 'I Believe you know quit as much as I do For I have Nobody to Come Near me', he said. He promised to write to his cousin, Richard, too. 'If Richard thinks he Can Be of Any use to Benefitt the case I should Be very glad of is Assistance', wrote Edmund, 'as I should Be very glad if he [or] Aneyone would assist me to git out of this place'. James Davenport had been ill and Edmund expressed his concern; he would write more often, but postage was expensive and he was allowed very little to support himself.

It was a misfortune in more ways than one that old James Davenport's health was 'declining so much'. His evidence on Edmund's behalf would be required at the ejectment trial.

* * *

Some time in July or early August 1835 Edmund Davenport informed his uncle in Middleton that 'my trial of the Rit of Ejectment is to Be tryed at Chester and you will be subpenied as Evidence in my faviour and to prove my Clame'. Old James Davenport must therefore think hard and do everything possible to help. Could he produce any old family Bible that had names written in it? Did he know any elderly person who had heard William Davenport of Bramhall acknowledge Edmund as a relative? What had James's grandfather, Samuel Davenport, said? What had his sister (Edmund's aunt) said? Edmund urged his uncle to remember anything that could be of service to him. A 'person', he said, would call on James Davenport (presumably to explain the details of procedure and go through the evidence) and a solicitor would see him before he went into court. 'I have No More to say at present But Live in hopes of seeing you all again', Edmund's letter concluded, 'give my Love to all frinds and Except the same from your Eficionate Nephew Edmund Davenport'.

On Monday 17 August 1835 the ejectment case Doe d. Davenport v. Humphreys[16] was heard before Kings-Serjeant

Taddy, who was taking the civil side of the Chester assizes that summer. (The serjeants-at-law still formed the aristocracy of the English bar, and they were often given the opportunity to act in a judicial capacity by being included in the commissions of assize.) It is unlikely that Edmund Davenport would be at Chester; his presence was not required. The law did not allow an interested party to give evidence on his own behalf, for that was considered too great a temptation to perjury. Sir Salusbury, of course, was in a similar position, and thus the evidence of the two people who might be expected to know most about the matter was excluded. We can assume that either Thomas Sharpe or Peter Morrison would be there, though neither was called upon for evidence. A jury was necessary in a civil trial when the facts were at issue and, as befitted the status of the defendant Salusbury Pryce Humphreys K.C.H., there was a special jury drawn from gentlemen of the county of similar status to himself.

Mr Temple K.C., leading counsel for the 'lessor of the plaintiff', opened the case for Edmund Davenport. 'Mr E. Davenport [he said] although a man in humble circumstances, was the representative of one of the most antient families in the county, and claimed this property as the heir-at-law of the late Wm Davenport Esq. who died in the year 1829 without any legitimate issue'. This statement gives us the clue to the different approach being adopted on Edmund's behalf at this trial. In Chancery he had claimed to be heir in tail male under a settlement made by a former holder of the Bramhall estate; now he claimed as heir at law to the last possessor. An heir at law was the person to whom property would descend if the owner died intestate. His identity was decided according to the principles of primogeniture which, on failure of the lineal line(from eldest son to eldest son), provided for descent being traced through a collateral line (from a younger son), male kindred taking precedence over female. Persons who were illegitimate were, of course, excluded from the descent.

That Edmund was the heir at law of William Davenport Mr Temple proposed to prove by tracing the pedigree back to Peter, the common ancestor, and at this point he 'described the pedigree in the ascending and descending series'. It was a 'wise policy of law', he said, which allowed the 'testimony of

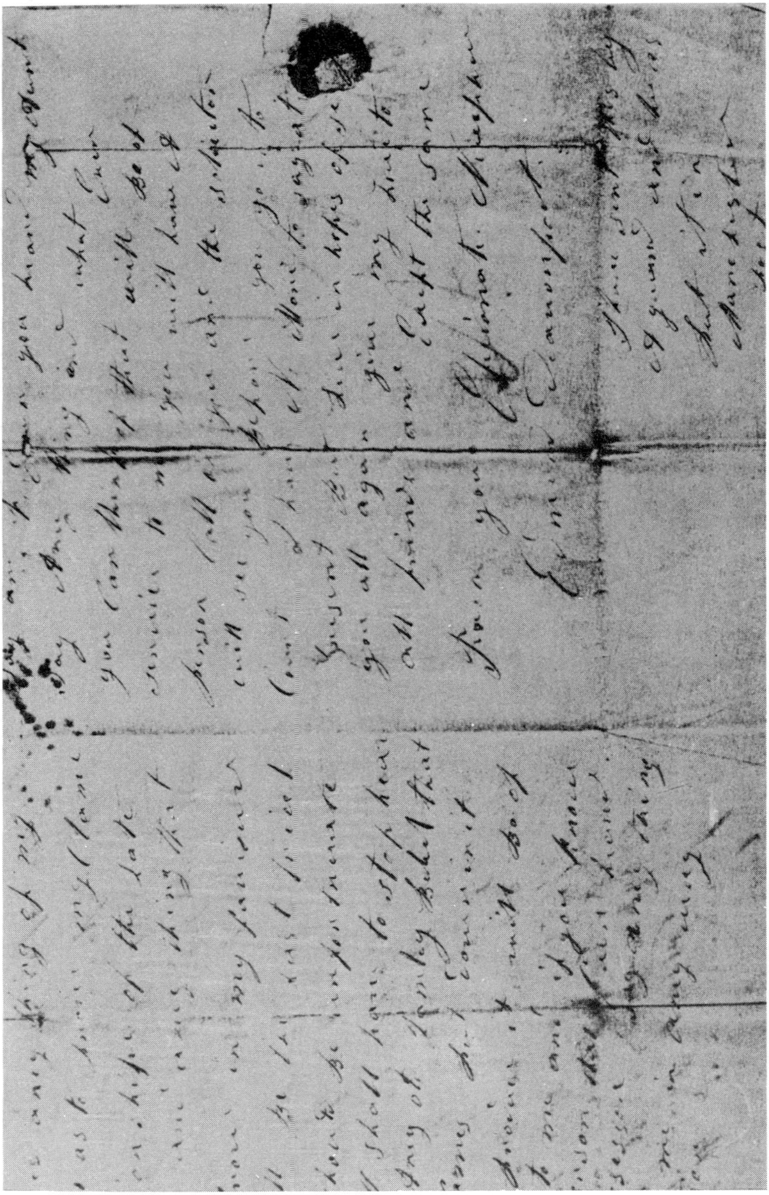

Edmund Davenport to James Davenport, (c June) 1835 (*Chetham's Library*)

reputation' when oral evidence was impossible (as in the case of persons who lived 150 years ago), and of such a kind would be the evidence of James Davenport, a man upwards of seventy years of age. He would state the history of the family as he had it from his elder sister Mary, who had it from their grandfather Samuel, who died when James Davenport was about six years old.

Counsel now turned to the descendants of the late William Davenport. Although married, William Davenport had no legitimate children, but he did have two illegitimate daughters, one of whom was married to Sir Salusbury Pryce Humphreys, the defendant in the case.

> Now if it could be shown . . . that the late Mr Wm Davenport gave the Bramhall Estate to his daughter, or to his daughter's husband, which it was perfectly competent for him to do, if it had so pleased him he (the learned counsel) would at once admit that the pedigree of his client, and his being the heir-at-law were of no avail: but if, on the contrary (as the plaintiff had strong reason to believe) the late Mr Wm Davenport, in addition to his manor and manor house had purchased sundry other estates and parcels of property, which latter he gave to his daughter or her husband, retaining the family estates for the Davenports – as was the constant practice with the old Cheshire families, who were proud, and justly proud, of transmitting the family estates in long lines of ancestry, from generation to generation – then would Mr Edward [sic] Davenport's claim to the property in question be clear and indisputable.

Here was a dangerous admission to make. Edmund Davenport always contended that it was not in William Davenport's power to give his estate to anyone; settlements and wills ensured that it must remain in the Davenport family. Why was an opposite admission made now? Was this the 'progress in discoveries' of which Thomas Sharpe had spoken? Edmund's advisers must have been convinced that Salusbury Pryce Humphreys could produce no valid deeds in his own defence; they had somehow been induced to believe that William Davenport bought other lands for his daughters and their husbands. The *Chester Chronicle* report of counsel's speech continues:

> If any deeds of the nature of those to which he had alluded were in existence, why were they not produced at once, and thus put an end to the case, instead of fencing and bush fighting at a long shot. . . .

> In most cases he (the learned Counsel) was free to admit, actions by heirs at law were no better than mere moonshine: but in the present case, where the descent would be proved, and the reputation in the family by a living member of it, the lessor of the plaintiff must recover, unless the defendant could show a better title.

Now came James Davenport's turn. He was called to give evidence of the 'tradition and reputation' in the family. His evidence was a dismal failure. Perhaps he was too old, or too ill, or perhaps he was scared by his unusual surroundings and the speeches of 'learned counsel', but he was unable to rise to the occasion. 'Even in his examination in chief, his testimony was very loose, vague and unsatisfactory with respect to the identity of *Thomas* . . . and this vagueness was still further increased in his cross examination', says the report. No evidence was produced from a family Bible, nor was there any written family pedigree.

Hugh Knowles of Bullock Smithy was then called, but his evidence was little superior to that of James Davenport. Knowles was required to produce examined entries of baptisms, marriages and burials from the registers of Stockport and Marple parishes, tracing the family of Davenport upwards from the last William Davenport of Bramhall who died in 1829 to the birth of Peter Davenport in 1622. 'In his cross examination it was elicited that he did not search the Registers very minutely to see if there were not other members of the family mentioned, but merely looked at those entries which had been pointed out to him'. In particular, Knowles admitted missing the record of baptism of Jenkin, Peter's second son, born in 1644, and his burial in 1688.

This ended the case for Edmund Davenport which, so far as we can judge from newspaper reports, was both ill prepared and ill presented. Sir Salusbury's counsel submitted that no proof of the marriage of Thomas had been attempted, nor of the identity of Peter, his father, from whom it was sought to trace the descent of the Blackley Davenports, and that in the absence of other genealogical evidence there could be no case for his client to answer. The judge would not go so far as this, though the facts were as stated, but requested counsel to go at once into his defence.

Mr Welsby, counsel for Sir Salusbury, then indulged in a

little sardonic humour at Edmund Davenport's expense before playing his trump card. He stated that:

> in a very few minutes he should put an end to the amusing *farce* of '*The Heir at Law*', which had been representing for the last half hour. The curtain of sad reality would very soon drop, once and for ever, over the ideal scene which the lessor of the plaintiff was wont to contemplate with so much fond delight, and over those pleasing prospects of Writs of Possession, and the receipt of the rents and profits of the Manor of Bramhall, in which he was so prone to indulge (laughter). His (the learned Counsel's) answer to the case was simply this: that the late Wm Davenport Esq, the father of Lady Humphreys, in the exercise of his undoubted right, gave the property in question to the present defendant; and as his (Mr Welsby's) learned friends were desirous to get a sight of the deed he would indulge their curiosity in that particular.

John Kenyon Winterbottom, solicitor for the Bramhall estate, then produced 'from the muniment room at Bramall Hall' deeds of lease and release[17] dated 10 and 11 October 1820, whereby William Davenport conveyed all his property in Bramhall and Stockport, his manor house and his manor of Bramhall, to Thomas William Tatton of Wythenshaw, to hold on various trusts, with remainder (after the death of William Davenport) to Salusbury Pryce Humphreys and his heirs and assignees for ever!

The jury immediately returned a verdict for Sir Salusbury. The editor of the *Chester Chronicle* was inspired to add a remark of his own to the reporter's account of the trial:

> Thus have 'vanished into thin air' the visions of *The Heir at Law* of Bramhall! Like many other claims of the same nature, his were indeed 'mere moonshine'.

Sir Salusbury Pryce Humphreys was amply confirmed in his possession of Bramhall. The verdict would no doubt be a weight off his mind, but he could hardly have considered Edmund Davenport as a serious rival. As with most landed proprietors litigation was part of his daily life; it was a job to be delegated to his solicitor, just as the management of the estate was delegated to his steward. Sir Salusbury's own place was on the bench, where he did not ask for justice, but administered it. Peter Morrison and Thomas Sharpe now drop out of the story. We have no clue as to the personal interest, if any, that either of them had in the result of Edmund's case, but whether their motives were entirely disinterested or whether they hoped for financial gain for themselves they were not prepared to go further. Sharpe, be it noted, could have felt both anger and amazement at the result of the trial. He had laid out money, time and energy on Edmund's case, and must have believed in it. He had been drastically misled, and may even have seen himself as being duped. His health was not good, for he suffered from recurrent bouts of rheumatic gout, and he died in 1838.

Edmund was shattered and bewildered. Thomas Sharpe must have withdrawn his support, for Edmund was now left with only the prison allowance, a small sum which each county paid towards the maintenance of its own poor prisoners in the Fleet. He now lived in 'The Fair', the very poorest quarters of the prison which could be rented. 'Bartholomew Fair' was the nickname which the inmates gave to the basement of the prison. It was 'down a dark filthy staircase, which appeared to lead to a range of damp and gloomy stone vaults beneath the ground',[18] and which Dickens's Mr Pickwick thought (until enlightened) were the little cellars where the prisoners kept their small quantities of coals! From No. 21 The Fair Edmund Davenport wrote imploringly to his friends.

Although he heard from no-one and was very badly off, Edmund still had thoughts of trying again. If it is true, as Edmund Davenport was later reported to have said, that the judge viewed William Davenport's conveyance with strong suspicion, ordering that a copy should be made for the use of Edmund Davenport and then recommending a new trial, it is not surprising to find Edmund writing to friends to try to raise money for another trial. Two such letters found their way into the hands of his cousin Will, who put them with Robert Andrew's pile of papers in the farmhouse at Woodhouses. Edmund had seen a solicitor (perhaps a fellow prisoner in the Fleet) who advised that William Davenport's deed should be examined, and Edmund himself was obviously overwhelmed that such a deed could have been produced in court. In October he wrote to his friend Robert Whittam, of Portwood (Stockport):

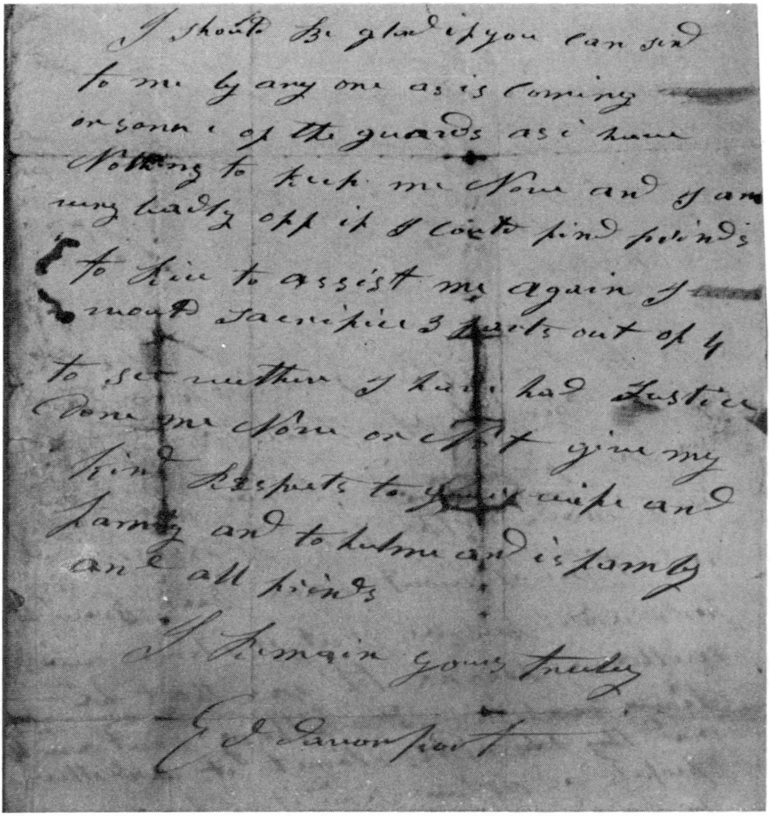

I should be glad if you can send
to me by any one as is Coming
or some of the guards as i have
Nothing to keep me Now and I am
very badly off if I could find friends
to hire to assist me again I
must sacrifice 3 parts out of 4
to see wether I have had Justice
Done me Now or Not give my
kind Respects to your wife and
family and to helme and is family
and all friends

I Remain yours truly

E Davenport

Edmund Davenport to Robert Whittam, 27 Oct., (1835) (*Chetham's Library*)

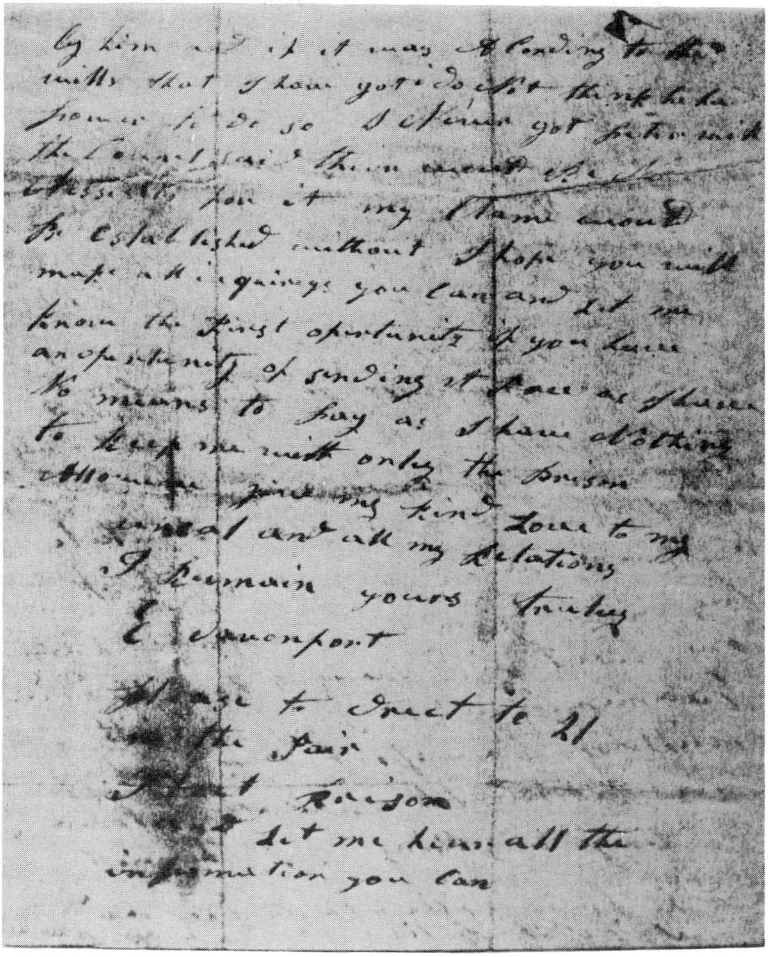
by him and if it may [illegible] bending to the
wills that I have got I do not think he he
power to do so I never got better with
the Counsel said then would be
necessary for it my Clame would
be Established without I hope you will
make all inquirings you can and let me
know the first oportunity if you have
an opertunity of sending it [illegible] as I have
no means to pay as I have nothing
to keep me with only the prison
allowance give my kind Love to my
[illegible] and all my Relations
I Remain yours truley
E Davenport
[illegible] to direct to 21
[illegible]
[illegible] Ransom
let me know all the
information you can

Edmund Davenport to 'Gorge wardel', 6 Nov., 1835 (*Chetham's Library*)

> I should Like to know the grinel opinion of the peopel A Bout this deed in my opinion if it had Ever been made in the Late possersers Life time it would have Been Brought forward Before But it Never was Willam Norme [William Orme, William Davenport's butler] told me that he Never wittnissed Nothing But a will and they have got is Name to it and other peopels as Never sined it I hope you will send me all the News you can if thier is any worth wile

This friend was evidently also a friend of James Hulme, the man who had defied Sir Salusbury over the rent of his piece of waste land and whose case seemed to have ended so triumphantly for Edmund. Edmund expressed surprise that Hulme had not written to him and asked whether it was true that Hulme had given up the land. Even so, Hulme was remembered in Edmund's final greeting:

> give my Kind Respects to your wife and famly and to hulme and is famly and all frinds

This letter and a similar letter written to 'Mr Gorge wardel Cheatham Hill near Manchester' the following month reveal Edmund Davenport's perplexity and the depths of his agony.

> Dear Frind [he wrote on 6 November 1835] I Received your Letter dated the 1 of this month and am very much oblidg to you for your information Respicting the trial at Chester it is very strange to me that my Frinds should give it up so Easy and Not Name A Bout the Entail as willams will of 17 hunderd and [? says] to my male hairs for Ever and several of the things as was at the hall is Named as Ever Lasting Legeseyses as hair Looms for Ever and they Never put that into the Brief att all I do Not know what to make of it I think if the deed was to be Examined that the Late posserser Never made it and I have been many times told that he Never could give it A way But I do Not know how they have made it up A mongst them they have got me hear and god knows when I shall get out I hope some Frind will [come forward] and see into it for me I would sacriafice 3 parts out of the 4 to find out wether I have had Justice done me or Not . . . No one Comes Near me I did Not think that I should have been Left in the way I am with onely the prision Allowance But I hope something will turn up for me after A while to Bring me on A gain . . . when I whent with willam Davonport to the hall the Buttler told me that he Never Sineyed aney thing But the will he knew Nothing of the deed and I do Not Belive it Ever was made by him and if it was ACording to the wills that I have got i do Not think he had power to do so I Never got peters will the [Court?] said their would Be No Necessity for it my

Clame would Be Established without I hope you will make all inquireys you can and Let me know the First opertunity if you have an opertunity of sending it free as I have No means to pay as I have Nothing to keep me with only the prison Allowance give my kind love to my uncal and all my Relations

I Remain yours truley
E Davonport[19]

Please to drect to 21
in the Fair
Fleet Prison

and Let me hear all the information you can

It is sad to see that Edmund dare not even ask for a reply to his letter unless it could be sent free (i.e. by private hand). Letters sent through the post must still be paid for by the recipient on delivery, and a letter from Manchester would have cost Edmund elevenpence.

Letters were then sealed, not put into envelopes, and there is a hole in the letter to Edmund's friend in Cheetham Hill where the seal has been broken open. Thus the last figure of the date of the will which Edmund quotes has been lost. Probably he was referring to the will of William Davenport of Bramhall who died in 1706 (grandfather of the last William), and his statement concerning the 'everlasting legacies' is correct, though it is not clear whether Edmund quotes this in support of an entail (the entail of Commonwealth days relied on in his bill of discovery?) or whether he believes the will embodies an entail. Actually the will is of personal property only, though it mentions a marriage settlement previously made which, it is fair to assume, would settle the estate on the eldest son. We wonder whether Edmund had seen the will of that eldest son, John, who was uncle to the last William and died unmarried in 1722. John, by his will, settled or resettled the estate on his two brothers and their sons, in order of seniority, or, failing male issue, on his sisters and their heirs. The last William Davenport, who actually inherited, was the only child of his generation to survive to manhood.

Edmund Davenport, in his private correspondence, puts his finger on the essential problem of the case. His perplexity remains our perplexity now. It seems impossible that the deeds set up against him could be other than genuine,[20] but if William Davenport did make them was he really entitled to do so? Today's evidence points to the answer Yes, although Davenports both of that time and later believed that the estate could not legally be given away. Why were Salusbury and Maria so reluctant to produce their documents? Surely they could have saved themselves the trouble and expense of court action and settled the case finally in their favour if they had shown their deeds to Edmund Davenport's solicitors, or, perhaps, to Thomas Sharpe? Why even in court did their counsel have to be pressed for this evidence, attempting first to show that his client had no case to answer? These and other questions crowd into the mind so that, although we may smile at Edmund's spelling and composition, we feel the rightness of his plea, made to each of his friends in almost the same words:

> If I could find frinds to Rice to assist me again I would sacrifice 3 parts out of 4 to see wether I have had Justice done me Now or Not

⋆ ⋆ ⋆

For some years after the failure of his ejectment case there was no change in Edmund Davenport's situation and, so far as we can see, no monetary response to his appeals for help. Sir Salusbury was now at the height of his success and power in Bramhall. In May 1838 he changed his surname to Davenport, dropping his other names and thus perpetuating the old family name at Bramhall. It was nine years since William Davenport's death and there was no obligation on him to do this. Neither William Davenport's deeds of conveyance nor his will made any such stipulation. The royal licence which granted to Salusbury, Maria and their family the authority to take and use the surname and arms of Davenport mentioned gratitude and affectionate regard for the late William Davenport as the reason for their request. Sir Salusbury Pryce Humphreys now became Sir Salusbury Davenport.

The affair of Edmund Davenport had not been completely forgotten in Bramhall, though it may have become a matter for jest and the raising of a laugh. About this time Hugh Knowles of Bullock Smithy entered into a wager with one of his friends or acquaintances concerning the marriage and death of Thomas, third son of Peter Davenport, and he wrote to

Edmund in prison requesting him to send documentary proof. It is interesting to note that Knowles, Edmund's agent in Bramhall who had searched parish registers for him, could not himself supply this proof. Nor was he to obtain this proof; Edmund replied that although he had such documents he saw no cause to furnish them in order to decide a wager.

Edmund's wife was very ill and she must have died soon afterwards. She had been a long time 'suffering dreadfully from a Cancer of the worst kind' and may have been taken to some free hospital outside the Fleet or to the home of a friend, for Edmund was allowed out twice to see her on her deathbed. (Permission for these visits had to be given by the Lord Chancellor; the authority of the warden was not sufficient.) During these years Edmund must have touched depths of misery and humiliation, but his spirit was resilient and by the end of 1839 he was again hopeful. His correspondence indicates that there could have been attempts to 'buy him off', for in a last letter to his uncle he declared that 'No one can suppose that I should be so great a fool and so unjust to myself to give up my claim to so large a Property descending from my Ancestors or that I would be bought off by him that has wronged me in so infamous a manner'.

That was in October 1839. Edmund Davenport was to be as amazed as everyone else the following summer by the spectacular crash of his opponent's chief agent, the solicitor whose business it had been to ensure that Edmund was safely lodged in prison, and then to buy him off, if buy him off he could.

III
TRANSPORTATION FOR FORGERY: the case of John Kenyon Winterbottom (1)

'What strange things occur in this extraordinary world – Winterbottom . . . who paid £10 to capture me has now £200 reward offered to any one that will capture him. . . .'

Edmund Davenport to a friend, 8 August 1840

In the long list of the mayors of Stockport the name of John Kenyon Winterbottom appears twice. For two consecutive years, in 1831–2 and 1832–3, he was mayor under the manorial constitution of the town. His office, dignified by ancient custom, was the highest position that the old borough could offer one of its citizens. The mayor wore 'a double chain of silver gilt, without badge or inscription, provided by the Lord of the Manor', and the two constables had similar chains and 'two walking staves, with massive silver heads'. During Winterbottom's term of office there were added to the town's insignia 'two small ebony maces, with ornamented silver heads, inscribed, 'Manor and Barony of Stockport, J.K.Winterbottom, Esq., Mayor', and bearing also the names of the two constables and the date, '1832'.[1]

The duties of the mayoral office were not considered onerous, real power being vested in the constables, but during Winterbottom's mayoralty there occurred an event – a landmark in the history of the town – which required more than nominal attention. As mayor he was called upon to supervise the first parliamentary elections and to act as returning officer. The great Reform Act of 1832 allotted two seats to Stockport, which previously had been unrepresented, and when the elections took place at the end of the year they proved to be a very rowdy affair. Captain Salusbury Pryce Humphreys (as he

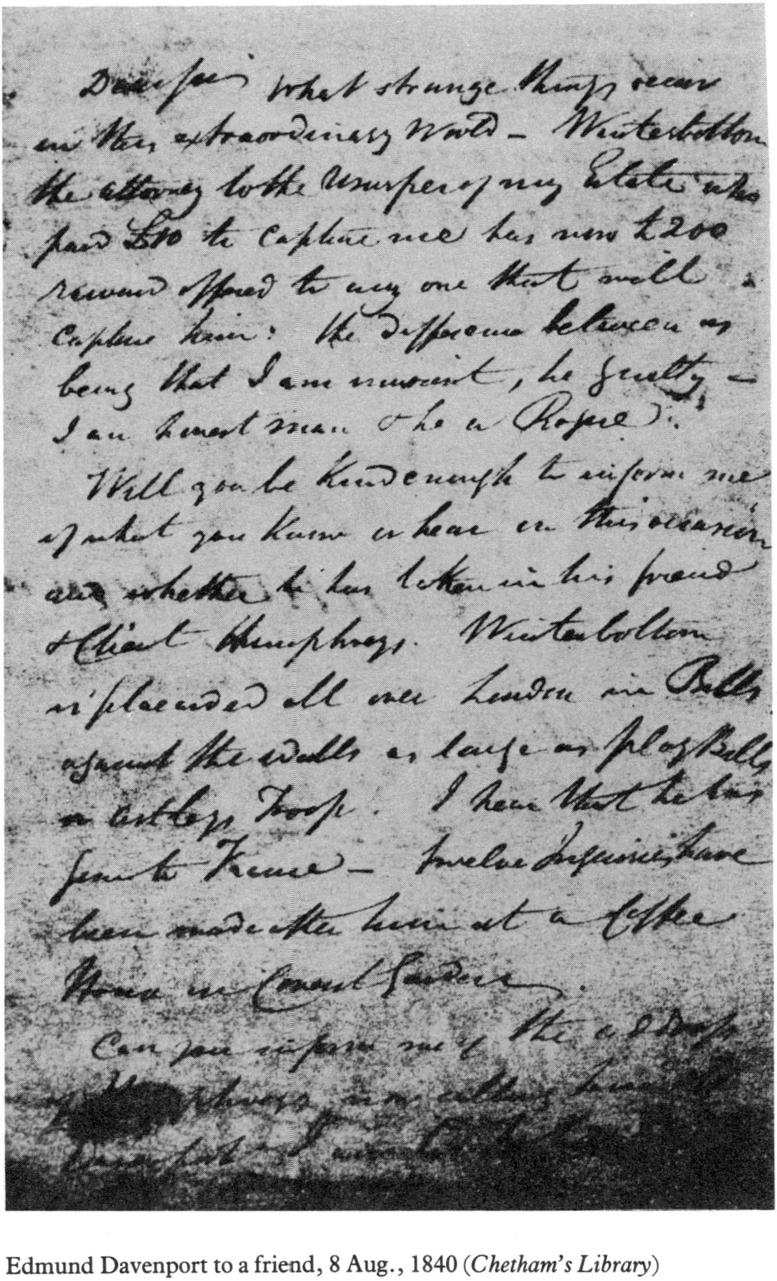

Dear Sir what strange things occur
in this extraordinary world — Winterbottom
the attorney to the usurper of my Estate who
paid £10 to capture me has now £200
reward offered to any one that will
capture him: the difference between us
being that I am innocent, he guilty —
I an honest man & he a Rogue!
Will you be kind enough to inform me
of what you know or hear on this occasion
and whether he has taken in his friend
& client Humphreys. Winterbottom
is placarded all over London in Bills
against the walls as large as play Bills
in an Artillery troop. I hear that he has
fled to France — twelve Inquiries have
been made after him at a Coffee
House in Covent Garden.
Can you inform me of

Edmund Davenport to a friend, 8 Aug., 1840 (*Chetham's Library*) then was) had seriously considered standing, but early withdrew his candidature on the grounds that 'the late hours of the House of Commons, together with the necessary absence each Session of four or five months from home, will not, upon more mature consideration, be in accordance with my pursuits and habits of life'.[2] Four candidates were nominated for the two seats, but a show of hands on nomination day did not suffice to secure an election. It became the duty of the mayor, John Kenyon Winterbottom, to arrange a poll, and during the two days on which it was held there was rioting and smashing of windows. The privacy of the ballot box was still many years in the future, and qualified electors (a minority of the population) were required to cast their votes in public. There were fights between supporters of rival candidates as well as intrigues between the candidates themselves, and although the mayor had arranged for five hundred 'special constables' from among the 'respectable inhabitants' of the town to join the thirty paid police to help to maintain the peace during the period of excitement, the military had finally to be called in to restore order.

John Kenyon Winterbottom was not born into the class of landed gentry (the 'burgesses' of Stockport's early-thirteenth century manorial charter) who, with the lord of the manor, had the duty of electing annually from among their number a chief officer, whom they called the 'mayor'. He worked himself up in the solicitor's office in which he served his apprenticeship, until he moved on equal terms with the town's top men. His business acumen was behind some of the most important ventures taken in Stockport. As well as acting as solicitor to many of Stockport's leading citizens he was also concerned with banking, an activity which until 1826 (when joint stock banks were permitted to set up in business outside London) was still entirely in private hands. Stockport had lacked banking facilities since the failure of a short-lived attempt to found a bank at the end of the eighteenth century, and in 1824 Winterbottom, with three partners, established what was virtually the first bank to be opened in the town. It traded under the name of the 'Stockport and Cheshire Bank', and its home was in Underbank Hall, the lovely old town house of the Arderne family, the purchase of which Winterbottom

Top: Blank cheque issued by the 'Stockport and Cheshire Bank', opened in 1824 (*National Westminster Bank PLC*); *Bottom:* Signature of J. K. Winterbottom on a bill of exchange, 1839 (*National Westminster Bank PLC*)

negotiated from the second Lord Alvanley at a price (so it was said) of three thousand guineas. Five years later the house was bought by the Manchester & Liverpool District Bank for their first branch in the Manchester area, and the banking business of Christy, Lloyd, Winterbottom and Worsley was amalgamated with it. John Kenyon Winterbottom continued to act as a banker for his personal clients, although his firm had been incorporated into the larger, joint stock bank.

By the 1830s Winterbottom was a man of means and a landowner. He was head of his very considerable legal practice, clerk to the trustees of several turnpike trusts, and attorney and confidential adviser to many of the leading gentry of town and country. He had also, at one time or another, held almost all the important public offices in Stockport under its old constitution.

The passing of the Municipal Reform Act in 1835 placed immediate extra responsibilities on J.K. Winterbottom, but the long-term effect was to rob him of authority and to decrease the power of the Tory oligarchy. For the period of the municipal elections he was appointed acting town clerk, and in this capacity he received official correspondence relative to the number of the new wards and their boundaries, and he drew up the revised list of burgesses eligible for the vote. No doubt he hoped that his own office would be confirmed after the new council assumed power, but in this he was to be disappointed. When the council met at the beginning of 1836 to elect its first corporate mayor and its first town clerk, Winterbottom was defeated by 29 votes to 9, the position of town clerk going to the up-and-coming young Liberal, Henry Coppock. Reform was letting in new blood to the government of the town. A few weeks later Winterbottom was also deprived of his job as clerk to the magistrates. This position was combined with that of town clerk, and with the two went a salary of £500 per annum! Even so, at the end of the decade John Kenyon Winterbottom was reputed to have an income of about £4000 a year, a very substantial amount at that time.

By the beginning of 1840 Mr Winterbottom must have presented the appearance of a typical affluent professional gentleman. He was fifty years of age (being born about 1790), short to medium height, rather stout and becoming corpulent. He had a thick neck and somewhat sallow face, with grey whiskers and light-brown hair, going bald. He usually dressed in a black coat and waistcoat, with checked or plaid trousers, and he walked with a short, quick step, and spoke thickly and loudly, with a pronounced accent. In retrospect it is not hard to see him as the strutting, well-dressed villain of a crime film.

Sad to say, he was indeed a villain; or, if the matter be put more kindly, he was tempted and he fell into crime. During the late 1830s he had been sinking more and more into debt, and by the end of the decade he faced financial ruin. He had lent too much on mortgage; he had speculated with investments and lost money. Herculean[3] efforts would not suffice to enable him to keep faith with his creditors and by July 1840 he could no longer stave off bankruptcy. His case was set down for hearing the following month before the commissioners in bankruptcy in Manchester but Winterbottom was not there to attend it. Worse charges now faced him and he had disappeared. That is why a description of his physical appearance has come down to us with such exactitude. An advertisement giving these details and naming him as a wanted man appeared on the front page of *The Times* on 8 August 1840.

* * *

Winterbottom had acted as confidential adviser to the Isherwoods of Marple as well as to, among others, the Davenports of Bramhall. In April 1829 he had been present at the funeral, in Bramall Hall chapel, of the last William Davenport of Bramhall, being one of the few gentlemen of the neighbourhood, close friends of the deceased, to be invited to walk behind the coffin. In May 1839 he occupied a privileged position at the funeral of John Bradshaw Isherwood of Marple Hall, for again he was the solicitor chosen to settle the family affairs.

Although John Kenyon Winterbottom had acted for the Isherwood family for years it does not seem as though he was actually engaged by them at the time of John Isherwood's death. The Isherwoods were a somewhat eccentric couple; the squire bluff, good-natured and honest, with just those little peculiarities of manner to add endearment, his wife morbid and over-sentimental in outlook. There may have been some difference of opinion within the family which caused

Winterbottom's services to be dispensed with for a time. However, he had already drawn up at least two wills for John Isherwood, the final will – made about 7 July 1838 – having been for some reason destroyed without the knowledge of the testator. Winterbottom had the instructions and a draft, and his help was therefore a necessity in proving the will. This he was engaged by the executors to do.

John Isherwood's son, on whom the estate was entailed, was not an executor. The boy was not yet quite of age, and he was of such a sickly constitution that he had not been expected to outlive his father. The four executors (then called 'executrixes' because they were women) were Squire Isherwood's wife and his three eldest daughters. An elderly gentleman, Mr Wilde, who lived at a distance, was also named as an executor, but he renounced the office almost immediately after John Isherwood's death.

One of the main assets descending to the executors was a capital amount of £5000 payable on a life insurance policy which John Bradshaw Isherwood had taken out years before. Winterbottom's duties included negotiating the payment of this money. After the funeral he was allowed access to the deed box at Marple Hall, and either on this occasion or some other, he took the policy into his own possession without mentioning the matter to the Isherwood ladies. In early December 1839 he obtained probate of John Isherwood's will at the Chester consistory court (probate being still the business of the ecclesiastical authorities), and on 20 December he presented the policy, with the necessary probate certificate, to Mr Tate, the Manchester representative of the Pelican Life Insurance Company, who had received instructions from his London office to pay the money. Remittance was made in the form of a bill of exchange (a forerunner of the modern bank cheque), payable to the four ladies named on the probate certificate in their capacity as executors. As the bill later became the subject of various legal quibbles, it is interesting to note the exact wording.[4]

£5000 Manchester, December 20th, 1839

At seven days' sight pay to Mrs Elizabeth Isherwood, widow, Miriam Isherwood, spinster, Anne Magdalene Isherwood, spinster, also Anna Maria Isherwood, now the wife of Charles

Bellairs, esquire, or order, the executrixes of the late John Isherwood, esquire, five thousand pounds, in full for loss under policy No. 11,012.

To the Trustees of the Pelican Life Office, London W.J. Tate

Mr Tate had at first omitted the words 'or order', thus ensuring that the money could not be paid to any but the four people named, but Winterbottom pleaded that this could cause difficulties, and at his request the words were inserted. Mr Tate made it clear, however, that the bill needed endorsing by the four executors in person; it could not be endorsed on their behalf 'by procuration'.

In early January 1840 Winterbottom sent the bill, with an accompanying letter, to the Bank of Stockport (not the 'District'), a joint stock bank founded in 1836 where he held a personal account. His letter requested that the money should be placed to the credit of this account. On the back of the bill appeared the 'signatures' of the four ladies (in writing not their own), followed by the genuine signature of J.K. Winterbottom.

It can be said at once that Winterbottom had himself written the names of the executors as well as his own name, for the fact was later freely admitted by his counsel. He had not 'forged' them in the popular sense of copying the exact handwriting of the persons concerned, but this was not necessary. Women, in those days of male dominance, very rarely had occasion to sign official papers. The handwriting of the executors would be unknown at the bank or in any similar place of business. Winterbottom merely wrote their names in four different styles of hand. No suspicion was aroused, and he almost immediately drew on his replenished bank acount to the extent of £2450. By the end of January nearly all the Isherwood money had gone.

As the year 1840 drew on Mrs Isherwood and her daughters began to make enquiries about the insurance policy. Winterbottom hedged. He told them that the document was in London. The money was not yet paid, he said, but interest would be allowed. Pressed further, he said that the Cheshire probate of John Isherwood's will was not sufficient to obtain the insurance payment; it was necessary to obtain a Canterbury probate. (Probate was granted by the ecclesiastical court which had jurisdiction over the *whole* of a deceased person's property, the highest court, covering every diocese in England, being the Prerogative Court of Canterbury. If it could be justly argued that the insurance policy was 'property' in London and not in Cheshire there might be plausibility in Winterbottom's claim that a Canterbury probate was required.) By the spring of 1840, so the Isherwoods later claimed, they were anxious to remove their affairs out of the hands of John Kenyon Winterbottom, but they still had no suspicions that they were being robbed.

The climax came near the end of July 1840, just as the state of Winterbottom's financial affairs and his impending bankruptcy were being made known. Mrs Isherwood again asked him about the policy and expressed anger at having had no accounts from him. Their patience exhausted (or, perhaps, their suspicions aroused) the Isherwoods made enquiry through another channel, and they discovered that the insurance money had been paid out some seven months earlier. It was now the beginning of August, and Winterbottom was not to be found.

There was a report that he had taken a berth on the *President*, due to sail to New York on Saturday 1 August, and that he was in Liverpool on the morning of that day. Being recognised, he must have decided to forfeit his passage and return to Stockport, where he was last seen on Sunday 2 August. On that evening he was reported to have left his home in Heaton Norris, accompanied by his wife, and been driven in his carriage to Manchester. Near Liverpool Road Station (the first railway station to be opened in Manchester, then still on the outskirts of the built-up area) he parted from his wife, and from that time disappeared from sight. It could only be presumed that he left by train for Liverpool that Sunday night.

Meanwhile the Pelican Insurance Company had been alerted to the fact that the executors had not received their money, and they at once instituted enquiries. Their secretary went out to Stockport, but he returned without achieving much, and at the beginning of August Mr Bush, the solicitor to the London Bankers' Association (an organisation especially charged with the detection and punishment of forgery), took over the investigation. The bill of exchange was traced in its progress from the Stockport bank to the London bank of the Pelican Insurance Company, and closely examined. It was shown to the four Isherwood ladies, who were positive they had never seen it before, and declared that the endorsements were not their own. They also insisted that John Kenyon Winterbottom had never received any authorisation to endorse the bill on their behalf. Mr Bush applied to the Stockport magistrates for a warrant for Winterbottom's arrest. At first, it is said, the magistrates were so astounded and unbelieving that they refused to comply, but when the evidence had been fully laid before them they were compelled to grant the warrant. A police officer was then sent in pursuit of the missing man.

* * *

John Kenyon Winterbottom was not found. It was first believed that he had embarked under a false name on the *Arcadia,* which had left Liverpool for Halifax, Nova Scotia, on Tuesday 4 August. Then he was traced to London and Dover, and it was supposed that he had crossed to France. John Forrester, one of the two metropolitan police officers who signed the advertisement in *The Times,* went over to Paris to search for him, but returned empty-handed.

The advertisement appeared on Saturday 8 August, just one week after Winterbottom's disappearance, and it offered a reward of £200 for his apprehension. It made no secret of the fact that he was guilty of forgery, even though he had not yet faced trial. 'ABSCONDED', it read, 'since Saturday, the 1st day of August instant, after having committed several forgeries, and having also, it is supposed, taken with him several deeds and valuable securities, not his own property, JOHN KENYON WINTERBOTTOM, lately of Stockport and Heaton Norris . . . attorney-at-law and banker'. Note that the Isherwood forgery was not the only deception Winterbottom was believed to have committed; other cases were now coming to light, or were believed to be coming to light.

The people of Stockport were stunned by the sudden disgrace which had come upon one of their leading citizens. The *Stockport Advertiser,* the newspaper of the establishment, refused to publish any details, or names, when news of the deception first began to seep through to the public at the beginning of August. Not until the name of Winterbottom had been made notorious by national advertisement did it go into print on the subject. The *Stockport Chronicle,* a paper with radical sympathies, was not so reticent, but its article of 7 August concentrated on the misery and distress which the bankruptcy must bring to many people, coupled with the universal esteem in which the unhappy bankrupt himself had been held, an esteem which the newspaper shared, despite its differing political views. The paper refused to comment on hints of a more serious nature, though 'the Borough rang with a thousand rumours', as it admitted the following week. By that time there were placards throughout Stockport making the charge of forgery generally known, and for both newspapers the restrictions were lifted. 'We abstained last week from noticing any of the rumours afloat until they assumed some definite form', wrote the editor of the *Stockport Advertiser* on 14 August, 'and we now approach the painful subject with the greatest reluctance'. The *Stockport Chronicle,* in a long article of the same date, detailed some of the cases of fraud of which Winterbottom was believed to be guilty, adding, 'Many parties made him the sole depository of their surplus funds. Hence the multitude of sufferers'.

Factually, the *Stockport Advertiser* of 14 August copied the report published in the *Manchester Guardian* two days previously, but in a separate article it tried to explain, and in some part to excuse, Winterbottom's inexcusable conduct. 'No event has ever occurred in the town . . . which has caused so great a sensation as the insolvency of this unfortunate gentleman, and his disappearance from the place under circumstances and charges of so grave and appalling description', it commenced. The *Advertiser* then suggested some extenuating circumstances which, before they passed judgment, its readers should take into account. 'Moral courage', said that newspaper, 'is one of the rarest qualities with which any human being can be endowed'.

> Ten thousand men may be found who will confront death and physical suffering, in their most appalling forms, for one who has the 'moral courage' . . . to descend voluntarily from that station in society in which he has been accustomed to move, and exchange, whilst it was in his power to enjoy them a little longer, the respect and smiles and blandishments which are lavished upon the rich and prosperous, for the cold courtesies which await the acknowledged bankrupt. . . .

> It would be wholly unnecessary . . . to enlarge upon the excellent character which Mr Winterbottom has hitherto borne amongst his townsmen. . . . As a son, a brother, a parent and a husband, his conduct has been most exemplary, and the poor and destitute have lost a friend to whose generosity they never appealed in vain.[5]

Edmund Davenport, a poor man himself, but a poor man with ambition to be rich, would not have approved of that last statement. John Kenyon Winterbottom (albeit in the course of his duties as solicitor to the family at Bramhall) had hounded Edmund and his associates, procured his imprisonment, and tried to make it impossible for him to continue his lawsuit. Edmund, in the Fleet Prison, quickly received news of the reward offered for Winterbottom's capture, and on the very day that *The Times* advertisement was published he sent a letter to a friend in Stockport begging for more news.

> What strange things occur in this extraordinary world [wrote Edmund Davenport] – Winterbottom, the attorney to the usurper of my Estate who paid £10 to capture me has now £200 reward offered to any one that will capture him: the difference between us being that I am innocent, he guilty – I an honest man & he a Rogue.

Someone must have described to Edmund the 'Wanted' notices displayed in the capital and likened them to advertisements of London's famous circus, for Edmund told his friend, 'Winterbottom is placarded all over London in Bills against the walls as large as playBills or Astleys Troop'. There had been enquiries made for the wanted man at a coffee house in Covent Garden, but he was now thought to have escaped to France. Naturally Edmund's interest centred on the relationship between Winterbottom, the attorney, and one particular client, Salusbury Pryce Humphreys (now Sir Salusbury Davenport), and he asked his Stockport correspondent 'Will you be kind enough to inform me of what you know or hear on this occasion and whether he has taken in his friend & Client Humphreys'.

Had Sir Salusbury been 'taken in'? Edmund Davenport would soon find out that Winterbottom was suspected of robbing Sir Salusbury to the tune of some £16,000 (though this amount was unsubstantiated), for on 18 August 1840 *The Times* reported at length the accusations which the *Stockport Chronicle* had made. Two cases involving Sir Salusbury were particularly mentioned. Winterbottom was said to have kept for himself a sum of £6000 which Sir Salusbury had given him years before to repay a mortgage (paying the annual interest himself so that nothing was suspected), and also to have retained £1000 recently received from the Manchester & Birmingham Railway Company as compensation for land it required in Bramhall. Misappropriation of rents was also suggested. (Were the Bramhall tenants doomed to have their rents filched from them for illegal purposes?) Defying the law of libel, which was not quite so strict then, *The Times* stated positively: 'The *Stockport Chronicle* details some of the cases of fraud of which he has been guilty'. Even the reticent *Stockport Advertiser* (copying the *Manchester Guardian*) mentioned, without giving any name, a further case involving £3000, 'but not having heard the circumstances stated on any sufficient authority, we shall not detail them'.

How true was all this? It seems that a second charge regarding the unlawful appropriation of £3000 was expected to be made, but it was withdrawn. Winterbottom was only actually tried on the one charge concerning the Isherwood forgery, and it cannot with certainty be said that he was guilty of any other, though the evidence points that way. The accounts of Sir Salusbury's new solicitors have survived for this period, and they show that he spent whole days at the end of July and beginning of August conferring with his advisers on the dreadful state of his financial affairs. They lent him £250 for his immediate wants. Their accounts are very circumspectly worded, but phrases like, 'explaining that you had already paid in the principal money through Mr Winterbottom', and (apropos of the railway), 'we found that no satisfactory arrangement had been made',[6] are, in this context, very suggestive. It would be wrong to accept the *Stockport Chronicle*'s report as true in every detail, but that its main charges have some justification seems undeniable.

We do not know how Edmund Davenport reacted when he heard of these further, unproved, charges against John Kenyon Winterbottom, but we must ask another question: Could Winterbottom have 'taken in' Edmund Davenport too? Could he have forged William Davenport's deeds of conveyance? The moral fall of a man whose profession demands absolute honesty and integrity casts a shadow over his whole past. By the time of the ejectment trial in 1835 all three witnesses to William Davenport's deeds of conveyance were dead. Fifteen years had passed since those deeds were presumed to have been made, and in the ordinary course of events no suspicion would be aroused, but where suspicion already exists the fact that none of the witnesses could be called upon to verify their signatures seems just one more suspicious circumstance. Registers of burial of the three people concerned had been produced in court, but, so far as we know, there was no attempt at proof of handwriting. On the other side it must be said that a forgery such as the deed would have involved demanded a different technique from that which Winterbottom employed in his known forgery. He did not try to copy exactly signatures which would be well known and could be verified, but he did pass a legal document which he knew to be false, with intent to deceive. His proved dishonesty was entirely for his own gain and not for the gain of any client. Indeed, if the rumoured allegations are to be believed, John Kenyon Winterbottom had been systematically robbing Sir Salusbury Davenport with one hand at the same time as he lent him money on mortgage with the other! It is the sudden revelation of Winterbottom's true character which produces a total lack of confidence in his previous actions, including his dealings with Edmund Davenport.

When Winterbottom's financial affairs came to be investigated by the commissioners in bankruptcy it became apparent that his largest creditor (the one who had, in fact, instigated the bankruptcy proceedings against him) was the Manchester & Liverpool District Bank, that bank whose Stockport branch he had helped to found. Rumour had it that he owed the bank anything between £35,000 and £80,000, but most of the debt was covered by securities and when these were taken into account the bank's claim was under £8000. At meetings of creditors in August and September 1840 debts to a total of about £29,000 were proved against Winterbottom, but most of them were of comparatively small amounts, many of the heavier claims not yet having been put in. Sir Salusbury Davenport, for instance, through his new solicitors, was still assessing his losses and for months the investigations dragged on. Sir Salusbury had borrowed money on mortgage from John Kenyon Winterbottom, and he also claimed money from him. Counsel's opinion was sought 'as to the £6000 professed to have been paid off by Mr Winterbottom',[7] the assignees in bankruptcy not being willing that this amount should be included in the bankruptcy accounts, and Sir Salusbury's claim was not finalised until October 1842, when his 'proof' was admitted for £3500.

Needless to say nothing was seen or heard of John Kenyon Winterbottom during this time, and after due notice had been served at his home address and forty two statutory days allowed for him to put in an appearance, he became liable to an indictment for felony and outlawry, in addition to the forgery charges already outstanding. He remained at large for just over four years. A veil must be drawn over his activities during this period, though it was later reported that he had been in France for most of the time, returning to Liverpool in the summer of 1844. Here he was very soon recognised and apprehended. A man named William Paine, a singer in public houses in Liverpool who had once followed a similar occupation in Stockport, was returning from bathing off the north shore near Bootle (that place being then a popular bathing resort), when he met and recognised Winterbottom. After they had passed, Paine consulted with his companion, informing him that £200 reward had been offered for Winterbottom's arrest. The other man proposed that they should 'have a go', but Paine hesitated. Finally he agreed, and they both set off in pursuit. Winterbottom took to his heels; the others chased after him. Winterbottom vanished round a corner, and after a short search his two pursuers had to admit that he was lost to them. They gave up the chase, and were retracing their steps when they met Policeman Lawson, to whom they told their story. Lawson took up the pursuit with the others, and they spent some time thoroughly searching a farmhouse nearby until they found Winterbottom crouching between a wall of the house and the shippon. Lawson told him he could consider himself in custody, and he was taken before the commissioner of police at the High Street Police Station. Here it transpired that the Liverpool police themselves had no instructions as to a charge against Winterbottom, but the commissioner directed that he should be sent to Stockport, provided that Paine, his captor, would take the responsibility. Paine, therefore, with his prisoner and the police officer, left Liverpool by train for Manchester. They missed the last train to Stockport, so took a coach and arrived at the Stockport Police Station about a quarter past eleven, Winterbottom being taken into custody for the night.

> He was miserably clad, the soles of his shoes being completely worn away, and he looked very ill and emaciated. He lay on the forms in the police-office all night, and [the following morning, Friday 6 September] after breakfast, which was procured him from the Bulkeley Arms, he was accommodated with fresh clothes, and was visited in the superintendent's room by [various Stockport] gentlemen, with whom, in the days of his prosperity, he had been intimately acquainted.[8]

Later that day he was taken before two of the town's magistrates, and remanded in custody, because the charge of forgery, brought four years earlier by Messrs Robarts & Co., the bankers to the Pelican Insurance Company, was still outstanding. One week later he was committed for trial.

Winterbottom must now have been almost penniless. Some said that when he absconded he had taken with him a considerable amount of money (though the *Stockport Advertiser* maintained he had made no provision for his flight), but when he returned he was destitute. 'He was reduced to such a state that his subsistence was dependent on casual charity', said *The Times*. That paper called him 'a melancholy personification of a fallen man'.[9]

Whilst awaiting trial he was lodged in Chester gaol. Although still called the 'Castle' this was a comparatively new building, bearing no resemblance to the old Norman castle on whose mound it stood. The embattled walls of the old castle had been taken down at the end of the eighteenth century in order to make way for an imposing group of new buildings, including the specially-designed assize court and the county gaol. They had greatly impressed a traveller of 1835.

> The gaol is on the new construction, the governor's house being in the centre, from which *vistas* radiate in every direction. The house is elevated above the cells, whose roofs spread beneath in the foreground, and in the distance a superb view appears of the

> surrounding country. On entering the turnkey's door, the healthful airiness of the prospect, and the cleanliness and tidy arrangement within the building, render it difficult to reconcile to the mind the contrasting emblems of solitude and imprisonment.[10]

Compared with many of the gaols of the time Chester sounds almost luxurious, and though prisoners could hardly be expected to appreciate the 'superb view', Winterbottom would probably experience less hardship here than he would have done almost anywhere else. He had been in prison only a few days when he was visited by Sir Salusbury Davenport's new solicitor, Mr Vaughan, requesting the assignment of a trusteeship in the Bramhall estate which he still legally held, and from his cell in Chester gaol Winterbottom duly executed the deed in favour of his successor. No doubt this was not the only piece of business he was required to transact in order to straighten out the affairs of his former clients.

On 8 December 1844 he was brought for trial. The visiting judge for the Chester winter assizes was Sir John Gurney, a baron of the Exchequer Court, much respected as a man but with a reputation for severity as a judge. On that December morning the places in court reserved for the public were densely packed ('with respectable persons from this and surrounding counties') for Winterbottom's case had attracted a great deal of attention. People were then inclined to patronise the courts of law as a form of entertainment analogous to the theatre, and they expected their favourite advocates to entertain with suitable rhetoric or a show of sentimentality. (Sir Salusbury's counsel, it will be remembered, had called Edmund Davenport's ejectment trial 'the amusing farce of *The Heir at Law*', and had managed to produce laughter at Edmund's expense.) Winterbottom's friend and counsel for his defence, John Jervis, was known as a great card player, and he could delight the public with his knowledge of card-sharping, among other criminal activities. (Jervis's own future career was not entirely without blame, but he survived the storm – a matter of election bribery – and ended up as Chief Justice of the Common Pleas.) On the present occasion humour and card-sharping were out of place, but Jervis was to play on the emotions of his hearers instead. Prosecuting counsel, the attorney-general for the county palatine of Chester, also knew Winterbottom well, and both sides vied with each other in extolling his virtues and his previously blameless character. Sorrow at the fall of a friend and colleague of such high standing, combined with resolution to put the truth of the matter at whatever cost to himself, formed the theme of the attorney-general's speech; Mr Jervis concentrated on the crushing effects of bankruptcy on his client. Many that day must have felt a pang of pity for the prisoner, who was dressed in black and came in looking 'exceedingly pale and distressed'.[11]

There was no denying the facts of the case as stated by the prosecution, but did they add up to the crime of forgery as defined by law? Not according to Mr Jervis. The prisoner, he claimed, coping with 'deep pecuniary embarrassment', believed he had a general authority to receive money on behalf of the Isherwood family, and, being tempted, he fell, and applied the money to his own uses. This could be called embezzlement or breach of trust (for which Mr Winterbottom was not at that moment being tried), but it was not forgery. He had not imitated the signatures of the executors, he had merely written their names on the bill, followed by his own. He had not absconded because his wrongdoing had been discovered; he had left Stockport ('driven from the town' was Mr Jervis's phrase) because he was unable to stand up to the investigation of his bankruptcy. He left to avoid the exposure of his affairs, and the pain this would cause to wife and family. 'Unfortunately Mr Winterbottom's mouth is closed or he would be the expounder of his own intentions', said Mr Jervis. 'He is precluded from giving such a clear explanation of the matter as he is well able to afford'. This was true. Like Edmund Davenport, Winterbottom was forbidden, as the interested party, to enter the witness box.

By the time Mr Jervis had finished his defence a halo surrounded the character of J.K. Winterbottom. He was 'the friend of the poor and the protector of the innocent'. On just this one occasion had he fallen from grace; he had misapplied a client's funds under the impression that he had authority to receive the money. 'The crime of forgery must be complete to satisfy the terms of this indictment', said Mr Jervis, and he pleaded that the jury could not possibly convict in such circumstances.

Baron Gurney was not impressed. Although elderly, and now in ill health, he was a strong judge, not to be influenced by rhetoric on either side. He had already remarked to the jury that if the evidence they were to hear proved the facts stated, there did not seem to be any doubt about their duty. Now he directed their attention back to the facts of the case. 'Really it is most alarming', he concluded, 'to find a professional man putting forged names to bills for the purpose of obtaining other people's money, and then turning round and saying, "O, dear, I thought I had authority to do this or that". It appears to me that all the fine character which has been given to the prisoner, he being a professional man, only makes his crime the greater'.

After such a summing-up the jury quickly reached a verdict of 'Guilty'.

Sentence was not immediately pronounced as Mr Jervis had earlier raised various legal matters connected with the form of the indictment which the judge, Baron Gurney, had said he would consider later. These were not suitable matters for the jury; they were technicalities of law which must be decided by the judges themselves. 'Judgment respited', said Baron Gurney, making it plain that the legal objections would be brought before the judges during the following law term. For the time being, therefore, Winterbottom was returned to the care of the constable of the castle at Chester. His trial, which had lasted five and a half hours, had taken less time than expected, though it still seemed long for those days when criminal proceedings tended, on average, to be more quickly (and less carefully) disposed of than they are today.

In the middle of February 1845 the various legal objections raised on his behalf were duly considered by the common law judges sitting together at Westminster. There was at that time no appeal against a criminal conviction, and Winterbottom's only hope of reversing the judgment lay in finding a technical error in his trial. To the lay mind most of the objections seem of a trifling nature. The indictment had stated that John Kenyon Winterbottom had forged the name of Anne Magdalene Isherwood with intent to defraud the Pelican Life Office; that he forged her name with intent to defraud the four (named) executrixes, and that he forged her name with intent to defraud various other people. One objection raised was that there was no such institution as the Pelican Life Office (although, as the reader will see, this name had been copied from the bill of exchange); it was the Pelican Life Insurance Company. Another objection concerned the number of the executors; there were five, not four, although one had not acted. Various further objections were put forward concerning the other people named as 'defrauded', but these quibbles were soon set aside. The matter on which the case hinged was that the indictment accused the prisoner of forging *one* name only on the bill of exchange – the name of Anne Magdalene Isherwood – whereas the bill needed four signatures in order to be valid. One signature alone could not have transferred the property in the bill. Even this seems to be largely a legal quibble, for it had been freely admitted (though not legally proved) that Winterbottom had written all four. One wonders, in passing, why the name of Anne Magdalene Isherwood should have been chosen if only one name was thought necessary on the indictment. She was actually the youngest of the four executors, but she may have been considered the most likely to carry weight in the witness box. Her mother, Mrs Isherwood, was unpredictable and known to be very antagonistic to her late husband's solicitor; Magdalene, on the other hand, was complimented by Judge Gurney at the trial, who called her 'a shrewd sensible woman' who had 'given her evidence with great intelligence and fairness'.[12] Whatever the reason that her name only appeared on the indictment, prosecuting counsel claimed that the indictment followed the terms of the Forgery Act of 1830 under which John Kenyon Winterbottom was charged. 'If there is an indorsement which will satisfy the indorsement of any one of the executors, that is within the statute', he said. This point was quite extensively argued between counsel for the prosecution and counsel for the defence, and then

> The court [i.e. the eleven common law judges present] took time to consider; and afterwards held the conviction right, on the ground of any indorsement being sufficient.[13]

It merely remained to pass sentence of law on John Kenyon Winterbottom. Less than twenty years earlier 'uttering a forgery' (that is, offering as genuine, with intent to defraud, a piece of writing with legal significance which was known to be false) was among the offences legally punishable by death. It was still a very serious felony. No doubt Winterbottom, who understood the working of the law as well as his advisers, desperately hoped that one or other of his objections, trivial though they might seem, would save him and serve to mitigate his sentence. Now all such hope was gone.

He was sentenced on 1 April 1845 at the next Chester assizes. There was a little delay before he was brought into the dock, and he looked very low and dejected and seemed hardly able to stand. The judge (Mr Justice Cresswell, one of those present when the reserved points were debated) informed the prisoner that his objections had been duly considered and found to be 'unavailing', and that the forgery of the name of Anne Magdalene Isherwood was 'a forgery within the meaning of the statute'. He continued:

> It therefore becomes my painful duty to pass upon you the sentence of the law. . . . I need hardly say that there is scarcely any class of men who have more power for evil or for good than the attorneys of this country – scarcely any class of men are trusted to such an extent and incur such responsibility as they do. . . . I cannot but regard your case as one of the most aggravated in its complexion that I ever heard of, and the punishment must be in accordance with your offence. The sentence of the court is, that you be transported beyond the seas for the term of your natural life.[14]

Winterbottom was then removed from the dock, and to onlookers he appeared 'deeply affected on receiving judgment'.

* * *

He was so ill that he had to be taken to the prison hospital. That ever-faithful Tory newspaper, the *Stockport Advertiser*, revealed this fact a few days later, when it made a further impassioned plea for sympathy and help for Winterbottom. It mentioned the 'appalling effect' the sentence had produced upon him, the 'hardships and privations' he had suffered during his four years out of the country, and his 'bitter sufferings' now compared with those a person 'in a lower rank of society' might be expected to experience.

> A man moving in a sphere like Mr Winterbottom, has already

> suffered a most dreadful punishment by the loss of caste in society – the destruction of his extensive and lucrative practice – and yet, besides all this, if his sentence is to remain unmitigated, his punishment is only commencing; – he has still, at his advanced age [he was now about 54] to look forward to banishment for life and all the rigors that a sentence of transportation involves.

The newspaper urged that, in spite of the seriousness of the offence, there should be some remission of the sentence, and was sure that 'our townsmen and readers will rejoice with us to hear that there is a probability of Mr W's case being strongly recommended to the merciful consideration of the Crown'.[15]

On 22 April 1845 a public meeting was held in the *Bull's Head* inn, in the Market Place in Stockport, in order to memorialise the Home Secretary for mitigation of the sentence on J.K. Winterbottom. The meeting was attended by about two hundred people, mostly working men, and a committee was formed to draw up the petition and obtain signatures. Early the following month a deputation of three travelled to London with the petition, which they said contained upwards of 20,000 signatures and was 62 yards long, but they returned with the news that further documentary evidence would be needed, and time was running out as Winterbottom would soon be removed from Chester Castle.

He left Chester on 14 June for Millbank,[16] the great depot for sorting and despatching convicts. This prison occupied a low marshy site on the bank of the Thames near Vauxhall Bridge, and it was the largest penal establishment in England. In form it resembled a great wheel, with its six long pentagonal buildings (containing 1200 separate cells) radiating from the centre, and the whole surrounded by a high wall. During his nine weeks' stay here John Kenyon Winterbottom was the prisoner in Pentagon 5, Ward C and Cell 6. Originally planned in 1813 on the lines of Jeremy Bentham's 'Panopticon', Millbank had proved an expensive failure as a penitentiary, and by the mid-forties was being used as a receptacle for convicts who would otherwise have been sent to the hulks. No man stayed here long; the average time was between two and three months. The population of the place was always changing; hardened criminals came to Millgate from all over the country and iron discipline was necessary in order to maintain order. Unlike

Winterbottom, most men were not first offenders. During their stay the prisoners were employed making soldiers' clothing, biscuit bags and hammocks, as well as the regulation prison clothing worn by themselves. They were kept only so long as was necessary to classify them and to make up consignments for the convict ships and various penal settlements.

In view of a government decision two years earlier, Winterbottom's classification was a foregone conclusion. He would be sent to Norfolk Island, the British possession one thousand miles north east of Sydney which had earned the name in Australia of the 'Ocean Hell'. For a few short years from 1840 to 1843 (the years of Captain Maconochie, the superintendent of convicts who in thought was in advance of his time), this naturally beautiful island which was inhabited only by convicts and their keepers had not lived up to its evil reputation, and it might have been better for Winterbottom if he had been caught when his crime was first discovered and transported four years earlier. Maconochie had tried, with the scantiest support from the home government, to introduce a 'Marks' system of reformatory punishment, and under him Winterbottom would have had a chance, by the accumulation of marks for good conduct and hard work, to reduce his period of detention on Norfolk Island and earn a transfer and a new start in Van Diemen's Land (as Tasmania was still called). He would have been encouraged to cultivate his own little plot of garden and grow vegetables. He would have worked as one of a small group whose members must take corporate responsibility for their actions. But after the end of 1843 all this was changed. Maconochie had been recalled under the mistaken impression that life for the convicts had become too easy, and his successor, Major Childs, was expected to introduce a new regime. At the same time a system of 'probationary punishment', of which Major Childs would operate the first stage, was decreed by the Colonial Office. Under this system all prisoners with sentences of fifteen years or more, including those with 'life', must spend at least the first two years of their sentence on Norfolk Island, with hard labour. Good conduct could not lessen the period, though bad conduct might extend it. Convicts who had completed this gruelling period of punishment would then be transferred to a probation gang in Van Diemen's Land for one or two years. Here some two hundred and fifty to three hundred men would be hutted and quartered together, and employed driving roads through unsettled areas or executing other works of public utility. Next would come the probationary pass, and prisoners at this stage could engage in private service for wages, though they might at any time be called upon to account for the expenditure of the money they earned. Prisoners who successfully completed these three stages would qualify for a 'ticket of leave', or probationary pardon valid within the colony itself, but not outside. Finally – and this was to be always a matter of 'grace and favour' and never of right – there might be a conditional or even an absolute pardon. This scheme, which was intended both to punish and reform, was doomed from the beginning, for under the new commandant in Norfolk Island the initial stage resulted in such appalling cruelties and degradation as to take away many a man's humanity and make him little better than a beast. This was the life upon which John Kenyon Winterbottom was about to enter, and for the first two years at least his lot must inevitably be cast with the dregs of human society.

On the morning of 19 August 1845 (just four days before Edmund Davenport obtained his release from prison) Winterbottom was taken with other prisoners to be put on board the convict ship *Mayda*. The men were chained together in batches of about twelve, led out by the only gate of the prison (which faced the Thames) and marched under armed guard down to the riverside. Although the hour was early a sprinkling of people gathered to see the convicts embark, and this strange procession of men, in prison clothes not necessarily chosen to fit, must have presented a sad and frightening sight. Two vessels belonging to the Woolwich Steam-packet company were waiting to convey the prisoners down the river to the convict ship moored off the Royal Arsenal. About one hundred and ninety five convicts were put aboard the *Mayda* that day, all bound for Norfolk Island. 'Amongst the convicts [said *The Times* the following day] is a person, who, it is said, once filled the office of mayor of Stockport, but now under sentence of transportation *for forgery*. Norfolk Island is the most severe penal settlement belonging to Great Britain, and the greatest offenders are generally selected and sent to undergo their punishment at that place'.

After ten days moored at Greenwich the *Mayda* was ready for her five-month voyage to the other side of the world, a journey of 17,000 miles. Like most of the ships used for convict transport she was not a government vessel, but belonged to a commercial firm under contract to transport its human cargo to the Antipodes. There had in the past been dreadful conditions and many casualties on such convict ships, and a surgeon-superintendent, absolutely responsible to the government for the health and safety of the convicts, was now sent out with each ship. An armed guard was also provided. Compared with many similar voyages that of the *Mayda* must have seemed comparatively uneventful, with favourable weather conditions, regular mustering of the prisoners on deck several times a day, and a strict routine for keeping the prison below in a dry and clean state. Even so there were four deaths on board (including one woman, the wife of one of the guards, who died after childbirth), and there were many cases of sickness among the prisoners. The surgeon said he had never seen so many cases of constipation, and there were also a number of cases of fever. ('Fever' in this context usually meant typhus.) His usual treatment consisted of bleeding (sometimes two or even three times), purging, and cold applications to the head or a blister to the epigastrium. He considered the prison lofty and well ventilated and the routine not unhealthy, and he wondered whether the water could be to blame for the amount of sickness, though it was much the same type of water as was carried in other convict ships and in merchant ships in general. He was probably nearer the mark when he noted how much improved the prisoners' health became after the stop at the Cape of Good Hope, when they could be supplied with fresh meat, vegetables and soft bread. The diet was at fault; it was poor in quality and probably insufficient in quantity. During that part of the journey which lay through the tropics wine was given on alternate days, not as a luxury but as a stimulant to help the prisoners through the voyage.

At the beginning of 1846 the *Mayda* came in sight of Norfolk Island. By this time the health of the prisoners generally had improved, and the surgeon was able to report that they seemed no worse than when they had first embarked. Norfolk Island

The Jetty, Norfolk Island (*Archives Office of Tasmania*)

possessed no harbour, and there was only one place on the south of the island where, in suitable weather, a safe landing could be made, for treacherous reefs surrounded the island effectively hemming in the penal colony. The prisoners were taken off the convict ship in small boats, rowed out by convicts from the island, and the actual landing was effected (according to one account) by swimming ashore, or (according to another) by leaping into the arms of a rescue man on the jetty.[17] A group of convicts from the island, stripped to the waist and ropes in hand, were lined up on the landing stage to form the rescue party. Winterbottom was not among those who had suffered serious illness en route, and he successfully negotiated the landing – how, we know not. He must have been physically very strong. On 8 January 1846 he was transferred to the charge of Major Joseph Childs, commandant of the colony.

Childs, with his subordinate officers and military guards, had responsibility for the life, work and conduct of nearly two thousand convicts, about one quarter of them being known as the 'doubly-convicted'. These were prisoners who had already been transported to New South Wales for crimes committed in the home country and then were re-transported to Norfolk Island for further offences. They formed a very ugly nucleus of hardened criminals. The remainder were men who had been sentenced in England and sent direct to Norfolk Island. As an administrator Childs was incompetent; as a disciplinarian he was cruel and unpredictable. Conditions in the prison were shocking, immorality was rife, and torture and floggings commonplace. By May 1846 Childs was losing all control, and reports of his dreadful régime filtered through to the home government. Inevitably there came a revolt among the prisoners; on 1 July a final provocation sparked off mutiny, and a section of the convicts ran amok, indiscriminately killing and injuring their guards. The rising was put down with harsh retribution. Speedy trials and hangings followed in quick succession. The island had sunk to the lowest point in its evil history and Stockport's ex-mayor was doomed to be among its convict population.

IV
IMPRISONMENT FOR DEBT: the case of Edmund Davenport (2)

'I arrived safe in London . . . and ever since then have been with Edmund . . . his being in Prison is a terrible thing and he must be got from there under some consideration or other as he is a old man and if he dies there the property will never be recovered . . .'

Will Davenport of Woodhouses to his wife,
1 July 1845

'When the search is completed it will be put in proper order for Councel and the Solicitor has no doubt of a favourable result'.

Edmund Davenport to his daughter,
8 July 1846

The year 1840 saw an outburst of activity in the lives of all the Davenports. Sir Salusbury Davenport, burdened with mortgages and perhaps also failing in health, was looking for a tenant for Bramall Hall. The defection of John Kenyon Winterbottom, his solicitor, had fallen very hardly upon him and opened up a chasm at his feet. Will Davenport in Woodhouses and Richard Davenport in Blackley were actively pursuing the family claim, while Samuel, Will's elder brother, also evinced a personal interest in the case. Edmund, in the Fleet Prison, was commencing intensive efforts to free himself.

By this time Edmund had found friends – probably fellow-prisoners – who would write his letters for him. Perhaps his eyesight was deteriorating, and certainly his compositions were not very literary (as will be seen from previous quotations). He must always have found letter-writing difficult and from about 1837 onwards all his letters were written for him. When, therefore, Edmund's cousin Samuel Davenport of Blackley wrote to him suggesting proceedings that he (Samuel) might take as next in line in order to obtain the rights which their family claimed, Edmund passed the enquiry to a fellow prisoner, a man of better education than himself. Richard Perkins of 'Top Gallery' (a prison address superior in more ways than one to 'Bartholomew Fair') may have been a solicitor himself, for it was not unknown for professional men to find their way into the Fleet. He claimed a full knowledge of Edmund's affairs, having perused his documents and 'set forth' his case. He wrote to Samuel on 20 August 1840 advising him to take joint proceedings with Edmund 'on the basis of a just and honorable understanding', but though this seems a reasonable proposition if the two cousins were at one in their view of the claim, Samuel did not take it up.

There must have been a very attractive side to Edmund's character (although he was a man of one idea) for he seems to have been able to make friends who were genuinely willing to help him rather than the type of false friend who would play on his yearning for wealth. Richard Perkins was one of the these, but his most famous friend was Richard Oastler, the factory reformer, who was committed to the Fleet in December 1840 for a debt of several thousand pounds which he had asked to be allowed to pay off in instalments. There were political reasons behind Oastler's imprisonment, but his enemies were unable to silence him. During his four years' internment Richard Oastler wrote and published his own weekly periodical, the *Fleet Papers,* in which he continued his campaign on behalf of the poor of the manufacturing districts. Edmund Davenport, by his own wish, was to appear in its pages.

Before the end of 1840 a suitable tenant for Bramall Hall had been found in the person of Robert Chapman Sharp of Manchester. He took the property furnished on a seven-year lease and Sir Salusbury Davenport and Dame Maria removed to Cheltenham, where they remained until Sir Salusbury's death over four years later.

During 1840 it had become known that Edmund Davenport would be putting in a petition for his release, and Sir Salusbury had to make sure that no release was possible without reference to himself. He gave instruction to this effect to the warden of the Fleet Prison.[1] His solicitors interviewed Edmund in prison,

Sir Salusbury Davenport (1778–1845) (*Metropolitan Borough of Stockport*)

offering him his discharge if he would undertake to bring no more actions for possession of the Bramhall estate. This Edmund would not do. Nor would he agree to put his case before the Insolvent Debtors' Court. In theory any poor debtor could petition this court for release, hand over whatever assets he had to the assignee of the court and be allowed to go free, the assignees making a distribution of his assets for the benefit of his creditors. Edmund would have none of it. He consistently refused to part with his 'papers'. Once through the Insolvent Debtors' Court he saw no hope of carrying his case further, and he was probably right. The law, however, gave Sir Salusbury a further weapon. As creditor, he could apply for an order vesting his prisoner's effects in the Insolvent Debtors' Court, and this he proceeded to do. The order was served on Edmund Davenport in March 1841, and the warden of the Fleet spoke to him about it, but nothing could shake Edmund's resolve. He was now looking forward to the petition for his release.

The following month Edmund obtained a little nation-wide publicity at Sir Salusbury's expense. Richard Oastler published an article on Edmund's case as a postscript to his issue of the *Fleet Papers* on 17 April. It concluded:

> It would seem that England is a hard taskmaster! It is 'too bad' that one of her defenders should perish in prison, and be deprived of his rightful property, at the bidding of an usurper, merely for the want of a few pounds to prosecute his claim! Such however is the case. I publish it at his request, in the hope that some plan may be discovered to enable the old veteran to obtain his rights!

Edmund, be it noted, was now nearly seventy. We do not know whether or not there was any public response to the plea for money implicit in his cry for help, but he must have impressed Oastler with his story. As a sign that Oastler did not later retract and become disillusioned with Edmund's case it is worth noticing that he mentioned Edmund again (not this time by name) two and a half years' later when they were both being transferred to the Queen's Prison.[2]

Now commenced a series of attempts on Edmund's part to obtain his release without paying the costs (or the full costs) owing to his rival. Every attempt failed. First he petitioned that he had been wrongly imprisoned under the name of a person called 'Edward' Davenport, not 'Edmund'. A discrepancy had been found in the office copy of the attachment which led to his imprisonment; no more, probably, than a copying error on the part of a writing clerk, but sufficient to provide a legal quibble on which to found a petition. In June 1841 Lord Cottenham, the Lord Chancellor of the day, heard and dismissed the petition. He decided that the error was a clerical one and the plaintiff was rightly detained under the correct entry in the registrar's book. It does not sound as though Edmund's counsel did very well for him on this occasion, for he remarked (either at the hearing or later to Sir Salusbury's counsel) that he had satisfied himself his client was not entitled to his release; it was his own fault he was in prison!

A year later Edmund tried again. At the same time he commenced proceedings which could lead to another ejectment trial. Notices were sent out in March 1842 to the tenants of the Bramhall estate, claiming the property in his name, but first an application seems to have been made to Sir Salusbury Davenport's solicitors for a settlement. They were advised that an offer of £200 p.a. made to Edmund Davenport before the previous ejectment trial would now be accepted. Was this just a preliminary gesture between solicitors to see whether the matter could be settled out of court? Was Edmund Davenport ever offered money if he would give up his case? Did he ask for money in return for abandoning the claim? The records are diametrically opposed here and no fair judgment is possible. All that is certain is that both sides refused to be bribed! Sir Salusbury, and later Dame Maria, declared that they had never promised anything and never would.

Sir Salusbury, in Cheltenham, could not have been very pleased to know that his tenant at Bramall Hall, Robert Sharp, had received notice that he should pay rent to Edmund Davenport! A conciliatory letter had to be sent to Mr Sharp. Edmund's notices paved the way for another declaration in ejectment which followed in October 1842, and during the intervening months his second petition for release was heard. This time it came before Lord Lyndhurst who had succeeded Cottenham on the change of government, but the views of the new Lord Chancellor were no more favourable to Edmund Davenport than those of his predecessor. He very quickly disposed of the old argument (brought forward again) that Edmund had been imprisoned under the wrong name. To this, however, had been added another plea – that no person granted permission to sue *in forma pauperis* ought ever to be imprisoned for costs – and this point was argued by counsel on both sides for over four hours. Edmund lost here because a definite order of the court had been made that he should pay costs up to the time of being admitted to sue *in forma pauperis,* and pay them he must. 'He has not obeyed the orders of the court', said Lord Lyndhurst, 'and therefore was attached for a contempt'.[3]

During the spring and summer of 1842 the Queen's Prison Bill was passing through Parliament, and at the end of the year all the debtors from the Fleet and Marshalsea prisons were removed to the old Queen's Bench (King's Bench) prison in Southwark. Conditions in the debtors' prisons had become the most scandalous in all the prisons for there was no discipline or control, the law requiring only the actual bodily confinement of the debtors. The Queen's Prison, as it was now to be called, was put under the control of the Home Secretary, who would be responsible for its efficient organisation. The idea had not yet been fully accepted by Britain's parliamentary leaders that the system of imprisonment for debt was wrong and useless, but the actual number of persons confined for debt was fast diminishing. When the removal actually took place in November 1842 not many more than seventy prisoners were transferred from the Fleet. Many were induced to take their cases to the Insolvent Debtors' Court and thus obtain their release, but some of the most hardened and longest-lived residents of the Fleet were most reluctant to leave, either for the Queen's Prison or for the world outside.

Edmund Davenport's case was brought before a judge before the transfer actually took place. This may have been part of a general review of prisoners being transferred, or it may have been another effort on Edmund's part to obtain his release before the transfer began. Sir Salusbury, as usual, opposed, and both sides were represented by counsel, but when it came to the point the judge refused to intervene as Edmund was now definitely in prison for contempt of court. He, like Richard Oastler, was duly transferred to the Queen's Prison.

Wretched conditions awaited the prisoners there, for the

authorities had not had adequate time for preparations and the poor debtors were treated like criminals. New regulations were being formulated which would limit visiting hours, part husbands and wives, and 'classify' prisoners. Richard Oastler hated it. His new room in the Queen's Prison, supposed to be one of the best, was swarming with bugs, and he had to pay £5 to have it cleansed. Edmund Davenport's room was probably one of the worst and, if he is to be believed, he had not £5 in the world. He could not have relished the move, even if his army experience had inured him to atrocious conditions. However, his ejectment case was going forward, and he must have been hopeful.

As soon as the declaration in ejectment was received[4] Sir Salusbury's solicitors made a detailed examination of all aspects of the previous ejectment trial (with which they had not been concerned) and then advised their client to apply for a court order restraining Edmund Davenport from proceeding further with his action until he had settled the costs of the 1835 trial. For some reason these costs could never have been demanded. Meanwhile Edmund Davenport, unaware that his opponent was planning to add to the burden of his costs, was trying to rid himself of that burden by making an offer of part payment of his debt. Where the money came from on this occasion goes unrecorded, but presumably Edmund had again found someone to help. On 19 November 1842 his agent called on Sir Salusbury's London agents and offered to pay the amount of £31 19s 7d if they would grant Edmund Davenport a final discharge. The amount offered represented only the costs of the Chancery suit in 1831; Edmund also owed £33 12s 6d for the costs of the demurrer (a total of £65 12s 1d). No discharge was promised, but Sir Salusbury's solicitors were willing to accept the money in part payment and give a receipt for it. Thereupon the offer of any payment was withdrawn. This episode demonstrates the futility of the conception of imprisonment for debt. If you could be indefinitely confined for a smaller sum as for a larger, why pay anything until you were certain you could pay the whole?

Both sides were now working furiously against each other. Edmund Davenport put in another petition to the Lord Chancellor for his release from prison. Sir Salusbury served on him the certified order for costs in respect of the 1835 trial. Edmund tried to have his petition put before either the Vice-Chancellor or the Master of the Rolls; Sir Salusbury ensured that it should be heard by Lord Lyndhurst, who had heard and dismissed the previous petition and, of course, dismissed the present one.

Sir Salusbury Davenport had gained an almost complete victory. Only in one respect had he been unsuccessful. He had applied for his costs of the Chancery hearing, but these Lord Lyndhurst refused to give as Edmund Davenport was still a pauper. This prompted Sir Salusbury's advisers to consider the possibility of dispaupering Edmund. If he could be deprived of the advantage of suing *in forma pauperis* he could be made to feel the effects of costs again. A final petition on Edmund's part caused them to act. Once more Edmund tried to petition the Vice-Chancellor; once more Sir Salusbury's solicitors took steps to ensure that the petition should be heard by Lord Lyndhurst. In the resultant confusion it was put on the agenda of both the Lord Chancellor and the Vice-Chancellor, but finally (on 1 April!) it was heard, and again dismissed, by Lord Lyndhurst.

Now commenced that collection of evidence which Sir Salusbury hoped might lead to the dispaupering of Edmund Davenport. His solicitors discovered a certain Mr Wenham, from whom they tried to obtain information concerning Edmund's circumstances. They interviewed Mr Wenham on five separate days in the early part of May 1843, and paid him £1 0s 0d, but ultimately they found that the information was not 'of that decisive character' which would justify an application to the court to dispauper. From the cryptic wording used by Sir Salusbury's solicitors we may safely assume that Edmund Davenport really was the very poor man he professed to be, and that he possessed no money of his own with which to prosecute suits or pay costs. However, from the point of view of Sir Salusbury Davenport, Edmund was safely in prison, and there he stayed without (so far as we know) further incident for two more years.

* * *

Now Will Davenport of Woodhouses enters the story again.

He wrote to his cousin Edmund towards the end of 1844 asking for information about the case. Edmund replied on 5 November, in a letter carefully put together by some friend. He assured Will that he had all the documents necessary to prove his claim; he needed to be set at liberty to be able to proceed. He had a copy of the original grant of land from the Crown, with inquisitions, wills and other documents concerning the Davenports of Bramhall for over five hundred years. (Edmund, like George Webster and Richard Davenport, seems to have put his faith in a mediaeval 'royal grant' to the Davenport family, but there he was wrong and hopelessly out of date. His legal advisers based his claim either on an entail of Commonwealth times or on the law of primogeniture.) Edmund told Will about the vesting order in the Insolvent Debtors' Court. He had not complied with it, although his opponents had threatened to have him sent to Newgate unless he did, and he was now, he said, 'under great privations'. He told Will that he possessed a copy of the deed brought into court at Chester and that three counsel had given an opinion that it was not valid. 'You may depend upon this Statement', Edmund's letter concluded, 'altho I have been 10 years in prison – and could long since have had my discharge, had I complied with their wishes'.

Six months later Will wrote again to tell Edmund that 'Captain Humphreys' had died. (The cousins seem to have found it difficult to remember that Sir Salusbury was now legally a Davenport.) The news greatly surprised Edmund, who seems to have been very much abreast of affairs in some ways, although in others he lived in the past, or, perhaps it would be more accurate to say, in an idyllic future. He asked Will to check the information. It was, in fact, premature, for Sir Salusbury Davenport lived for another six months. He had what was then called 'senile gangrene' (a degenerative condition of the arteries) and he could by that time have been seriously ill. Will had written to the Heir-at-Law Society concerning Edmund's claim, and they had asked for his papers, but Edmund, cautious as ever (should we say wily?) would not part with them. He had already discovered that the chief manager of the society was often in prison himself, and indeed might be in the Queen's Prison even while he was writing!

Edmund asserted again to Will that the opposing parties

would discharge him, and provide for him, if he would give up his claim and take no more proceedings to recover the property. How right was he here? It is an open question. Evidence from the other side suggests that only a few weeks earlier Sir Salusbury had received (and refused) another request for money; his solicitors had declared that it was 'delusive' of Mr Davenport to expect Sir Salusbury to give him anything for renouncing his claim; it was within Mr Davenport's own power to discharge himself from prison at any time.

In the early summer of 1845 Edmund saw what he called 'a fair chance to get my liberty' and he asked for Will's help. 'It behoves you to do all you can for me', he wrote on 17 May 'as you may be in possession of my papers [does he mean in the event of his death?] for if any of the documents I have are lost they can never be obtained again.' Edmund believed (quite wrongly as it turned out) that unconditional freedom would make everything easy for him. At the end of June 1845 Will Davenport journeyed to London to see his cousin. He took a lodging at the Free Trade Coffee House in Friar Street (off Blackfriars Road) where he would be handy for the Queen's Prison on Borough Road. He found everything as Edmund had said, and he agreed to go into the matter jointly with him.

For a day or two Will went about Edmund's business in London. He was greatly impressed by Edmund's numerous papers and documents ('he has the Christenins and Burial of all the family and the whole are of the greatest satisfaction to me'); he saw men of the law with Edmund every day, and he felt sure he must succeed. On 1 July Will wrote again to his wife in Woodhouses, but this time the letter was written for him by the same person who had written earlier on Edmund's behalf. 'I arrived safe in London . . . and ever since then have been with Edmund and am going backwards and forwards about the Town every day since on his business and a good deal I have for to do for him still before I leave London . . . his being in Prison is a terrible thing and he must be got from there under some consideration or other as he is a old man and if he dies there the property will never be recovered'. But by now Will had spent all the money he had brought with him, and Edmund was too poor even to provide him with food. Here was the crunch of the matter. Will begged his wife to send money as soon as she could

– no less than £1 – 'and I shall make no more away than absolute necessity requires'.

The reply which was sent the next day from Woodhouses was short and to the point. It was written by Will Davenport's eldest son, a young man of about twenty one. He enclosed £1 for Will to come home 'and not to expend it in going about after the case any longer'. Edmund's case was obviously not very popular in Will's home at Woodhouses. 'Besides my mother is taken ill', added young William, 'therefore you must make the best of your road home we cant send any more by no means whatever'.

So ended Will's personal connection with Edmund's case. On 23 August 1845 Edmund Davenport obtained his release, but there is no evidence that Will had anything to do with it. Somehow Edmund obtained the money to pay his debts. His release was attended with certain behind-the-scenes formalities. A guarantee was requested from Sir Salusbury that, upon obtaining payment in full, he would withdraw the vesting order of 1841 and consent to his prisoner's release. He replied that he had no objection to Edmund Davenport's discharge. What else could he say? Theoretically he was concerned only with receiving payment for debts justly due. Then followed a little ceremony before the Vice-Chancellor, Sir Lancelot Shadwell, the judge who had first awarded costs against Edmund in 1831. Solicitors for both parties met at Lincoln's Inn on the appointed day. Finding that the Vice-Chancellor was not sitting that day, they travelled down to his home at Barn Elms, the old manor house of Barnes. Here, in the presence of Sir Lancelot, the total costs of £65 12s 1d were paid over to Sir Salusbury's solicitors, with an extra amount of £1 7s 4d to cover the costs he incurred taking out the writ of attachment. Sir Lancelot made an order for the discharge of Edmund Davenport, and Edmund was at last free! He had been in prison 10 years 38 weeks and 4 days.

Sir Salusbury had not mentioned the vesting order; that remained to be dealt with by Edmund Davenport himself. His solicitors agreed to offer no opposition provided that Edmund paid the costs himself, and this he was obliged to do. On 14 October 1845 the vesting order was cancelled. Edmund expected the costs to be £6–£7, and he had just received money from some source, as a letter to another cousin (not Will of

Woodhouses) shows. In the event, Sir Salusbury's bill of costs amounted to £14 6s 0d, but when checked and certified by the taxing master it was reduced to £8 1s 0d, which amount Edmund paid. 'They gave me all the trouble they could', he wrote. 'I am now thank God quite free from them'.[5]

Edmund Davenport's dreams of an easy entry to at least part of the Bramhall estate did not materialise. The reality was very different. He found himself homeless in a new, changed London, with only such money as was sent him by relatives and friends. The railway companies were now pushing their lines towards central London, demolishing whole areas of slum property on the way, but thereby making the housing problem even more acute for the poor who could not afford to move to the suburbs. By October 1845 Edmund had found a temporary home at No. 10 Arundel Street, Strand, a lodging house in a district of lodging houses, and the particular room (or part of a room) which he occupied had been lent to him by a friend. 'Had I not met with a friend who kindly lent me a lodging while absent I must have slept in the Street. I expect my friend to return every day', he wrote to his daughter in July 1846. He was very badly off and desperate for help with money. Yet his case (he said) was still going forward. A certain Mr Powell, who could read old handwriting and knew some Latin, was searching the records in the British Museum on his behalf and also the newly-sorted papers in the Tower of London which were now being made available to the public. 'When the search is completed it will be put in proper order for Councel and the Solicitor has no doubt of a favourable result', wrote Edmund. But the real purport of his letter was to convey his own desperate plight. 'I have no lodging to go to till I hear from someone', he said.[6]

Sir Salusbury Davenport died in Cheltenham on 17 November 1845. By a very simple will, made a few weeks previously, he left everything to his wife, Maria. No particular property was specified – the name of Bramhall never even mentioned – but Maria inherited everything he possessed. At the beginning of 1846 there was another intimation from Edmund's solicitors that he might now be inclined to accept an offer which had previously been made, but Lady Davenport was firm in her denial that any offer had ever been made. For

Dame Maria Davenport (1785–1866) (*Metropolitan Borough of Stockport*)

the present this silenced Edmund Davenport, but during the next two years her solicitors were required on occasion to dispel doubts concerning the validity of Maria's title, and this they were able to do to the satisfaction of the people concerned.

Edmund Davenport's next effort came in the summer of 1848. He petitioned the Lord Chancellor for his pedigree to be examined by one of the masters in chancery, and he pleaded his poverty. Lady Davenport opposed the petition and was represented by counsel; Edmund, it seems, appeared for himself! It was hardly to be expected that he would do well on his own with professional forces arrayed against him, and his petition was dismissed. Maria was awarded costs, but her solicitors thought it unlikely that these would be enforced in view of Edmund's previous status as a pauper. One month after this hearing they received a further 'application' as to whether any 'arrangement' could be made. They replied firmly that Edmund Davenport had lost his case at law and in Chancery and could expect no offer from Lady Davenport.

By the beginning of 1849 Edmund Davenport was again in a position to prosecute his cause. He now lived at No. 9 King Square, off Goswell Road, and he must have found some financial backing, though the disastrous result of his final effort leads one to feel that his latest sponsor, whoever this might be, was a man of straw. In January Edmund commenced an action of ejectment, and a little later another suit in Chancery. On the face of it the Chancery suit seems a little unnecessary; one feels that, in his precarious circumstances, Edmund Davenport (if he must take action at all) would have been better advised to concentrate entirely on the ejectment. It is ironic, too, that the Chancery suit, which caused his final ruin, came nearer to success than any he had initiated before. This time, instead of asking for 'discovery of documents', Edmund's chancery bill requested an injunction against Lady Davenport forbidding her to cut down and sell timber off the Bramhall estate until the result of his ejectment action was known at law. Granting an injunction was still the preserve of the Court of Chancery; like 'discovery' it was denied to the courts of common law.

Edmund's bill of 1849 was similar in form to his bill of 1831, but there was one curious difference. Instead of citing a settlement of Peter Davenport's father, it cited a deed of Peter himself, made at the end of December 1656 and enrolled by fine in the Court of Common Pleas in Hilary Term 1657. This deed was said to be between Peter Davenport (on the one side) and Thomas Legh and Edward Hyde (on the other), the latter two gentlemen being, presumably, Peter's brother-in-law, of Adlington, and his near neighbour, of Norbury. By it the Bramhall estate was settled on each of Peter's sons in turn, and in default of any such issue it went to the 'right heirs' of Peter Davenport.[7] It was under this last clause that Edmund made his claim. Four sons of Peter Davenport were named in the deed – William, Jenkin, Albin, John – but Thomas, surprisingly, was not among them. He had been baptised in 1645, the year after Jenkin, and if alive he would have been eleven years of age; hardly old enough to have left the parental home or to have been disinherited for any reason. Edmund's second chancery bill seems to support the supposition that Thomas died young.

Edmund did not think so. He claimed that Peter Davenport died in 1658 leaving *five* sons surviving: William, Jenkin, Albin, John *and Thomas*, 'the lineal ancestor of your Orator'. The old formula was then followed; Edmund's supposed pedigree as before, the entry of 'Sir Salusbury Pryce Humphreys Davenport' upon the estate, and later of his widow Dame Maria Davenport. Then came another surprising statement.

> And your Orator sheweth that your Orator did not discover his title to the said Estates and premises till within a very recent period.[8]

What did this mean? Did Edmund have new evidence which would be used in the forthcoming ejectment trial? Would William Davenport's deeds of 1820 be challenged? Or was this statement merely an apology for the length of time which had elapsed before the case was brought? We shall never know, for Edmund's petition was never heard. Dame Maria demurred, and her demurrer was allowed.

She obtained the best defence counsel possible. At that time the law officers of the Crown were still allowed to engage in private practice, and she retained Sir John Romilly, the Solicitor-General, son of a famous father (Sir Samuel Romilly) and himself destined to become Master of the Rolls in two years' time. She demurred 'for want of equity'; in other words, she claimed that the Court of Chancery had not the power to grant an injunction such as Edmund Davenport requested, and her demurrer was heard on 2 and 6 March 1849 by Sir James Wigram, one of the two additional vice-chancellors who had been appointed to cope with the ever-increasing volume of work in Chancery. Had it been left to his own discretion, Sir James would have granted the injunction. By her very demurrer Lady Davenport had in some sense undermined her legal position, for implicit in the demurrer was the admission that the statements in the bill *might* be true; she was merely claiming that they had no relevance in law. (This was the peculiar result of demurring and a risk that must be taken.) In these circumstances, if the question had never arisen before Edmund Davenport would have obtained his injunction.

But there was a precedent! There had been a similar case in 1817 and Sir William Grant, Master of the Rolls and a most revered authority, had then refused an injunction. Sir James Wigram would not take it upon himself to overrule such an authority. 'I must refer the Plaintiff to a higher tribunal if he thinks he can sustain the bill', he said.[9] In other words, an appeal must be made to the Lord Chancellor.

No appeal was made, nor was the ejectment action continued. Edmund Davenport was ruined by this case. Time was running out for him, for it was nearly twenty years since the death of William Davenport of Bramhall and after that time his right to bring any action would be extinguished and the title pass by 'adverse possession' to Maria Davenport. Even so Maria had made all preparations for her defence at the forthcoming Chester assizes. Documents and papers on which her title was founded were ready to be produced. Just before the ejectment action was due to be heard at the Chester assizes, Edmund Davenport (or his advisers) withdrew it.[10] This is what the *Stockport Advertiser* of 6 April 1849 had to say about it:

> This case which was entered early in the Cause List [No.7] was abandoned by the plaintiff early in the week. It was an assumed action on the part of some individual to recover, as heir at law, the possession of the Bramall Hall estate. On Tuesday [3 April], however, the record was withdrawn, and, on inquiry, it turned out that, although everything was fully prepared for the defence by the respected solicitors to the family of Lady Davenport, the plaintiff

> could never seriously have contemplated carrying the case into Court, inasmuch as no steps had been taken towards instructing Counsel, or any of the other necessary preliminary arrangements taken for the trial. It is rumoured in Chester, that the case was probably the offshoot of a conspiracy to extort money.

The reader must judge for himself the accuracy of that last remark.

★ ★ ★

Lady Davenport had, of course, been awarded costs in the Chancery case. She had costs arising from Edmund Davenport's original motion for an injunction and costs for her own successful defence by demurrer, and the total this time amounted to £93 18s 4d. No sympathy was wasted by Dame Maria on Edmund Davenport. Taxed certificates were at once obtained and she made preparations to have attachments issued.

First, payment of the costs must be formally demanded. Representatives of Lady Davenport's London solicitors prepared to do this on 4 May, but when they called at No. 3 Devonshire Street, Portland Place (the house where Edmund was now presumed to be living) they were informed that he was not there and that it was uncertain when he would be back. They arranged to call again at 11 o'clock the next morning. On the second visit a servant told them that Edmund Davenport was within, but when the mistress of the house appeared she declared that Mr Davenport had left Town and would not be back until Monday night. Another appointment was made for 11 o'clock on Tuesday.

Now the agents went to No. 9 King Square, Goswell Road, the address from which Edmund had issued his Chancery bill, and they found the house shut up. On making enquiries next door they were told that the occupants had left six weeks ago. Then they went to the home of the landlord in Vincent Place, and he assured them that 'the parties' had indeed gone to No. 3 Devonshire Street, for he had seen them there.

On Tuesday of the following week Lady Davenport's agents went to the house in Devonshire Street at 8 o'clock in the morning and waited (outside?) until 10 o'clock. They then saw Edmund Davenport leaving the house, whereupon they served him with the taxed order of costs and demanded payment.

Edmund replied that he could not pay as he had not got the money, but the woman who was with him said she had no doubt that the account would be paid in a day or two as Mr Davenport was not without friends. (Note Edmund's directness. It was his companion who tried to play for time.)

Lady Davenport did not delay. The warrants for Edmund's arrest were obtained on 16 May 1849, but now the London solicitors had to track him down again, for it was unlikely that Edmund would remain at No. 3 Devonshire Street. They found a man who at the instigation of Lady Davenport had been asked to help, and whose son knew of Edmund's whereabouts in London and would assist in his arrest. The son was interviewed, so that arrangements could be made. Even so Edmund was not taken for another six months. New attachments were issued at the beginning of December and Edmund was arrested and taken to Whitecross Street Prison just fifteen years after his first arrival there in 1834. This time it was a sentence for life.

Whitecross Street was a prison entirely for debtors. It served the City of London and county of Middlesex, and had been purpose-built thirty five years earlier. It occupied a site stretching through from the lower part of Whitecross Street to what was then Redcross Street, the old church of St Giles Cripplegate lying immediately to the south with the top of its tower visible from the prison yard. Even before the building was completed the plan was condemned by a committee of 1815 charged to report to Parliament on the state of the London prisons. In particular, the committee said of this 'New London Prison for debtors' that 'the placing of debtors in large communities in the sleeping rooms, is a great aggravation to the pains of imprisonment'.[11] By this time the building was too far advanced for alteration.

William Hepworth Dixon, a lively and popular writer of the time with a sensitive social conscience, himself conducted an investigation into prison conditions in 1850, and his description of Whitecross Street is a description of the place as it was when Edmund Davenport was there, and where he ended his days. The atmosphere was melancholy in the extreme; the poor debtor, said Dixon, could do nothing except waste his time. The day room was shared by every man in the ward and there

The Fleet Prison, (*Guildhall Library*)

was no privacy. 'Store room, cooking room, sitting room, dining room, reading room, and smoking room . . . it is necessarily full of many scents. . . . The gentleman occupies the same day-room and night-room as the vagrant. There is no distinction of persons in Whitecross Street gaol'. The bedrooms were 'arranged in long chambers . . . sixteen or eighteen in a room. . . . The bedrooms are all badly ventilated. . . . The water closets are in a disgraceful condition.'[12]

Edmund Davenport was 78 when he was arrested for the second time, and the census of 1851 showed him to be the oldest person in the prison. There were 180 male prisoners, twelve officers and their families, and seven servants. Edmund was still a widower, and he was also put down as an 'annuitant', probably indicating that he received the county allowance. If so his 'friends' had proved illusory, or no better off financially than himself, and he was in the ward which Hepworth Dixon found the saddest of all. Here, in the Dietary ward, were placed those persons who were unable to maintain themselves. The weekly ration Dixon considered liberal, but, he said, 'This ward is full of miserable objects; and the effluvia of tobacco, cooking and confined air in the day-room are almost overpowering'.[13]

As the years wore on Edmund Davenport became weak and aged. He spent some time in the prison infirmary, and he developed a chronic cough. Some time before his death he had 'a fit' (a slight stroke?) which affected his speech and one side of his face. On 20 February 1856 he had another fit – the prison surgeon said this was an epileptic fit – and during the night he had three or four more fits. He died the next day. On 22 February William Payne, coroner for the City of London, held an inquest in the prison. Although it was not yet a matter of written enactment that there should be an inquest on any person dying in prison it had long been a recognised requirement of the common law, and Payne was not the man to abrogate his responsibilities. A jury was summoned, and three people, including the prison doctor, gave evidence. They said that Edmund Davenport had received every care and attention. The coroner recorded his verdict. Edmund Davenport, aged 84, a prisoner in the Debtors' prison for London and Middlesex, being there sick and languishing, on 21 February

1856, 'by the visitation of God (to wit) of infirm old age and epileptic fits . . . died a natural death'.

The following year, 1857, a prisoner who preferred to conceal his identity under a pseudonym published a poem of many verses entitled 'A Voice from a Debtors' Prison'.[14] Its first verse may serve as an epitaph for Edmund Davenport, as well as for others like him.

They tell me that England belongs to the free,
That Britons will never be slaves;
Yet tyranny rampant, with sorrow I see,
Where prisons are sometimes their graves.

V
TRANSPORTATION FOR FORGERY: the case of John Kenyon Winterbottom (2)

'God reward the Just & the Right & punish the Guilty'

Edmund Davenport to a friend, 8 August 1840

Hepworth Dixon, that critical observer of the London prisons of 1850 whose description of Whitecross Street, the place of Edmund Davenport's death, has already been quoted, maintained that it was better to be a convict transported for seven or ten years than a debtor in Whitecross Street gaol. 'In Australia', Dixon wrote, 'by industry and good conduct, a convict may redeem himself, may recover a position and amass wealth'.[1] The emphasis is on the possibility of a new beginning rather than its probability, still less its certainty, and Dixon was thinking, of course, of a young man with a shortish sentence and his life before him. John Kenyon Winterbottom was not such a man, yet his later career can be used to illustrate the truth of Hepworth Dixon's words. Miraculously, so it seemed, he survived the terrors and rigours of transportation and became a free man again. The records are sparse, but they show that Winterbottom worked through the various stages of probationary punishment in little more than ten years, a far shorter time than the originators of the scheme had envisaged for anyone with a life sentence.

He lived through the mutiny on Norfolk Island and within eighteen months he was transferred to Van Diemen's Land. Here he was required first to undergo twelve months' heavy labour on a penal settlement, and he was sent to Tasman's Peninsula, some forty miles south east of Hobart Town, where thousands of convicts, in their various gangs, worked at tree felling and land clearance. Winterbottom is put down as a 'monitor', which seems to imply that he was given a degree of authority over some of his fellow convicts; not necessarily an easy or enviable position. There is a glimpse of him at 'Cascades' on Tasman's Peninsula in the memoirs of another convict, a literate man intent on telling the world about his fate. This convict remembered his fellow prisoners as a motley group of men, with a sprinkling of the educated in their ranks, and looking back to the year 1847 he wrote:

> Our society now became somewhat improved; for though I did not hear of any naval or military officers, barristers or doctors of medicine, I could count two Protestant clergymen convicts, one of them a doctor of divinity, several solicitors, including an ex-mayor and many chartists . . .[2]

He says no more about the 'ex-mayor', but as the author of this memoir was transported nearly two years before Winterbottom he would be correspondingly in advance of him in each stage of punishment. Their time at Cascades overlapped by, at most, a few weeks, as also must have their period of labour in Norfolk Island.

In September 1848 Winterbottom petitioned the Colonial Secretary, Lord Grey (through the governor of Van Diemen's Land) for some amelioration of his condition, alleging an illegality in his trial and the absence of any felonious intent on his part in committing the offence for which he was sentenced. In the state of transport at the time his 'memorial' took six months to reach Lord Grey and a further six months for a reply, so that it was just over a year before he knew the result; his petition was refused. Nevertheless he must have received some remission of sentence made possible by a combination of good conduct and good fortune. By now the system of transportation was becoming increasingly unpopular with the free colonists themselves, and the problems of absorbing the vast numbers of convicts who had been poured into Van Diemen's Land during the last few years were alarming. Winterbottom, like others, benefited from the governor's scheme whereby remission could be earned on a day-to-day basis by hard work and exemplary conduct. Three years after his first arrival in Norfolk Island he became a probationary pass holder in Van Diemen's Land, and he could now, under strict conditions, work privately for wages (if he could find work) or earn his living at Prisoners' Barracks in Hobart Town by stone breaking and other public labour (if outside work proved unobtainable). The records show him in Prisoners' Barracks at the beginning of 1849, prior to starting work for William Turner. During the next few years he worked for various employers, twice returning to William Turner. There is no indication of the type of his employment, or of the amount of time he actually spent in Prisoners' Barracks, but with his superior education Winterbottom could hope to find himself employed, during at least part of the time, in a clerical position. In 1854 he received his 'ticket of leave', giving him substantial freedom within the colony, and on 27 July 1856 he was granted a conditional pardon, allowing him every liberty except that of returning to the United Kingdom. He became a free citizen of Hobart Town, and in that year the foundations of the new state of Tasmania were being laid.

For a time Winterbottom seems to have worked with a whaling firm, but in the month of February 1857 he and a fellow employee of the same firm were involved in a drunken frolic, arrested and brought before the justices in Hobart Town for trial. The two men were found guilty of stealing a hat, the property of a third person, and they were each sentenced to one month's hard labour. The hat was found on the head of Winterbottom by the constable who apprehended him, and the hat's owner, who had just come from the public house much the worse for drink, did not even recollect losing it. The shipowners who employed Winterbottom and his mate must have considered them valuable employees, for they petitioned the Governor for some remission of the sentences which would allow the men to return to work, but the report of the Chief Police Magistrate was unfavourable and no remission was granted. It sounds a trivial and unnecessary case, out of character for an educated man of sixty seven, but then so were his circumstances and his job and the very society of Hobart Town (including the composition of the police force) which was heavily ex-convict. Happily for Winterbottom it was not many years before he was able to use his old skills again. About 1860 he was appointed Town Clerk and Treasurer to the Hobart Town Council and once more he occupied a position of special responsibility and trust. It would seem that his great talents

Town Hall, Hobart, 1866 (*State Library of Tasmania*)

were recognised by his employers, and he again had the opportunity to leave a mark for good on the municipality which he served. He was Town Clerk during the years of the building of Hobart's new Town Hall. It was described in a *Town Hall News Letter for Friends Abroad* (perhaps actually written by Winterbottom, certainly done under his auspices) as 'in the Italian style of architecture, producing some of the more striking characteristics of the Venetian school', and he became the first town clerk to have his office in the new building. At the Grand Ball, given by the Mayor in October 1866 to mark the official opening, Winterbottom, as was his duty, accompanied the mayor and aldermen in procession to the dais in the large hall, where, beneath the light of three magnificent crystal chandeliers bearing 84 gas jets, the fifteen hundred guests were formally received. There followed supper and speeches and dancing till the dawn of day. But for Winterbottom all was not well. He held his position for only nine more months. His downfall came in summer 1867.[3]

Winterbottom was now about seventy eight and ageing rapidly. He was not in good health, his memory was failing, and he appears to have been withdrawn and immersed in his own thoughts. His employers evidently recognised that the job had become too much for him, and asked for his retirement, offering to pay him a year's salary in lieu of notice. Before his retirement could take effect he was arrested for embezzlement. In his position as Town Clerk and Treasurer he had, of course, the handling of monies due to the Corporation, and his duties included the acceptance of money paid for debentures issued by the Corporation, and the payment of interest upon them. Winterbottom did again what he had so long ago been accused of doing with money entrusted to him by Sir Salusbury Davenport; he kept the money instead of applying it to the use for which it had been given, and he himself paid the interest in order to avoid suspicion. He kept £400 given him by Hannah Redfern of Hobart Town for a re-issue of debentures, and he himself paid her the interest on bonds which had never been properly issued by the Corporation.

His trial on 10 September 1867 before the Chief Justice of the island was almost a replica of his first trial in 1845, but on a smaller scale. The charge this time was not forgery, but the lesser one of fraud. Both sides stressed the painful nature of the proceedings, due to the prisoner's age, position and failing health, and the judge declared that his was the most painful duty of all – the duty to pronounce sentence on such a man. Yet 'the law has no respect of persons', as the prosecuting attorney-general said, and again there was no denying the facts of the case. All defending counsel could do was to 'explain the circumstances under which the unfortunate old man at the bar appeared before them', and this was not made any easier by the fact that the old man was unco-operative and had given his advocate no help. However, counsel was able to make some pointed remarks concerning the way in which the Corporation's accounts were kept and their peculiar method of doing business, asserting that 'It was a cruelty on the part of the Corporation to permit such a state of things, and to keep the prisoner in a position for which, owing to his age and infirmity, he was wholly incapacitated'. Apart from this the defence was limited to showing that Winterbottom might not actually have appropriated the money to his own use, although he certainly had not paid it into the Corporation's bank account. He might have kept it loose in a chest where some £320 not otherwise accounted for had been found in banknotes!

The jury brought in a verdict of 'Guilty', the judge commenting that they could have done no other, but they added a recommendation to mercy on account of the prisoner's old age. The judge then addressed Winterbottom at some length. 'I regret', he said, 'to see a man in the position you hold, at your age, and with, I am told, increasing infirmities, stand in the position you now occupy. But am I to be deterred from the strict course of justice by considerations like these? I am afraid not. Surely, surely, that very age, and those approaching infirmities and the experience of your long past life, surely those should be some guarantee and safeguard. They are not to be thrown to the winds. They ought to be some guarantee and safeguard against such acts as yours'. There was a convention that one did not make direct reference in public to an ex-convict's past, but the meaning is clear. The Chief Justice was also in a dilemma. He obviously feared that any sentence he passed on the old man before him might be a sentence of death, not life, but on the other hand he was concerned at the prevalence of fraud, not only in Tasmania (as Van Diemen's Land had now become), but also in the sister colonies. Ex-convicts formed a very large proportion of the population, and deception and fraud were only too common. The idea of punishment as a deterrent to others won the day, and the judge passed a sentence of two years' imprisonment on John Kenyon Winterbottom. Nor was he to be explicitly exempted from the hard labour included in the sentence. 'I am content to rely on the consideration of the Executive that no task will be imposed on you calculated to shorten your days', said the Chief Justice.

The first time he was sentenced Winterbottom had shown great emotion. This time he seemed hardly to be affected. He 'listened attentively to the remarks of the learned judge, but, apparently, without fully hearing or quite comprehending them'. The terms of his sentence had to be communicated to him by his counsel.

Why did he do it? No suggestion was offered at the trial, and the judge commented in his final address, 'I know not why – I know not when the temptation came, but you abused the trust and confidence reposed in you'. Was John Kenyon Winterbottom basically a man who could not resist the lure of money? Had he become so corrupted by the society in which for many years he had moved that he now hardly knew right from wrong? Or was he in some strange way regressing to that state of mind of nearly thirty years ago when, compulsively, he appropriated the money of one person to pay to another, in a desperate and futile attempt to satisfy his creditors?

Winterbottom had survived his sentence of transportation; incredible though it may seem he survived this sentence, too. His further two years in Prisoners' Barracks did not prove to be a sentence of death, as his contemporaries seemed to fear. He lived to be eighty three years of age, and died a free man 'at his residence' in Hobart Town on 17 May 1872. His death was announced in the Hobart *Mercury* next day: 'The funeral will move from St David's Church. . . . Friends will please accept this invitation as no circulars will be issued'. There was no mention of any family, but John Kenyon Winterbottom would have an honourable burial from the cathedral church at Hobart. Edmund Davenport, dying penniless in prison, might have had no more than a pauper's burial.

'God reward the Just & the Right & punish the Guilty', Edmund Davenport wrote from the Fleet Prison to his friend in the Stockport district when he heard of the Winterbottom forgery. On the face of it neither reward nor punishment seems to fit, though Edmund was thinking in terms of Old Testament justice; he had forgotten that the New Testament reminds men of the innate fallibility of all. Yet nearly one hundred and fifty years later Edmund Davenport has his reward. He emerges from this investigation as a man of integrity who commands respect; John Kenyon Winterbottom commands, at best, only pity. So it appears to the writer; others must decide for themselves.

VI
THEN AND NOW

Less than fifty years after Salusbury (Pryce Humphreys) Davenport succeeded the tenth and last William Davenport of Bramhall, the estate was broken up, and the building of what has since become commuter-land began soon afterwards. By 1850 the family had returned to Bramall Hall, and in due course the property passed to Colonel William Davenport Davenport (born William Davenport Humphreys), the eldest son of Salusbury and Maria. He died in 1869 leaving an only son, a youth of seventeen. In 1877, as soon as that young man became of age to inherit full rights under his father's will, he sold the Bramhall estate and left Bramhall for ever. When his title deeds were being examined one curious little defect came to light. Shortly before his death in 1829 William Davenport of Bramhall had acquired from the Road Improvement Commissioners a small strip of land on the north-eastern boundary of his estate, and this land was technically excluded from the legacy to his son-in-law. (Before the Wills Act of 1837 only that land owned by the testator at the time of making his will could pass by it). Whether they knew it or not Sir Salusbury and Dame Maria had indeed held one small piece of land illegally (a fact which would be well understood by John Kenyon Winterbottom, who had acted for William Davenport). The discrepancy was noted in 1877, and queried by the solicitors acting for the company purchasing the Bramhall estate. 'The 220 yards, Stockport Great Moor, conveyed to Wm Davenport on the 18th Feby 1829 descended to his *heir* his daughters being illegitimate. Who was such heir?' they asked. This was the reply:

> This small plot of land appears to have been held with the remainder of the property for nearly 50 years. The vendor, therefore, has a possessory title to it.[1]

Bramall Hall: east front today (*Metropolitan Borough of Stockport*)

If only this question had been asked earlier! It would at least have formed a basis for a true examination of the Davenport of Blackley pedigree, something which was never seriously undertaken by the law.

'I Shall eat my Roast Beef and Plumb Pudding at the Hall at Christmas and we shall make the walls Eco with mirth & Joy at its being once again in the Possession of its Lawful Lord & master', wrote Edmund Davenport in 1832.[2] He was wrong, of course. Yet the walls of Bramall Hall have echoed with much mirth and joy (and some sadness) since his time, and do so still. It is thanks to the efforts of two Manchester business men of the new industrial age, and not to any Davenport, that the manor house itself was saved from destruction and eventually found its way into the safe keeping of the local authority. In the summer months the sound of many footsteps can be heard throughout the building. They are the footsteps of members of the public who pass from room to room trying in imagination to picture scenes gone by. But concerning Edmund Davenport Bramall Hall is silent. It never knew him.

Nor, in spite of the many reminders within its streets, has the town of Stockport shown any desire to remember its former mayor, John Kenyon Winterbottom. A town likes to feel proud of its prominent citizens, and expects their lives to contribute to the good name of the place. In histories of Stockport Winterbottom's name has been mentioned only so far as his public offices and duties required it; he has then been quietly forgotten. Heginbotham, Stockport's major historian and himself an ex-mayor, only mentioned Winterbottom's bankruptcy (a state not necessarily deserving of moral censure and one to which private bankers of the early nineteenth century were particularly prone); yet he must have known very well the story of Winterbottom's flight from justice and his trial. Writing near the end of the nineteenth century when the records of the manor of Stockport had become scattered, Heginbotham was particularly anxious to trace the collection of ancient Court Rolls, some of which he had found in private hands. 'They are supposed to have been squandered when the Steward, Mr John Kenyon Winterbottom, became bankrupt in 1840', he wrote, 'the papers having been in his possession by virtue of his office'. Having made enquiry of the solicitors who acted under the Winterbottom bankruptcy, Heginbotham was told that 'about the year 1870, all the papers relating to the Winterbottom estate, except those of the bankruptcy, were sent to London to be pulped, and were therefore destroyed'.[3] It was really not to be expected that family or friends would wish them to be kept, and, so far as is known, no personal papers concerning John Kenyon Winterbottom have since come to light. Perhaps his spirit is most evident in Underbank Hall, that ancient black and white building in the centre of Stockport which he bought for a bank and which has remained in the same use ever since. It now belongs to the National Westminster Bank and is beautifully maintained. Wellington Road, that three-mile length of wide straight road, with its eleven-arch bridge over the Mersey, built in 1825–6 in order to bypass the steep and narrow streets of the town, is also partly his work. His firm acted as solicitors to the Manchester & Buxton Turnpike Trust which undertook the (then) tremendous task. Now that the day of the motor car has arrived the 'new road' has become so busy and so built up that a stranger travelling along it may be forgiven for thinking he has passed through the centre of the town! In June 1832, watched by a crowd of some twenty thousand people, Winterbottom laid the foundation stone of the Stockport Infirmary on a site on the southern side of the new Wellington Road. This building, like his bank, is still in use, and there are other memorials of John Kenyon Winterbottom still to be found in and around Stockport. He was a man of 'commanding talents and indefatigable industry',[4] and he could have been one of Stockport's great men.

There are other buildings of historical interest still standing which take us back in time to the lives of the people we have come to know, but I shall here mention only one. An old pottery kiln in the centre of Swadlincote marks the site of Thomas Sharpe's extensive pottery works. It is only the shell of one of his kilns, rebuilt in the later nineteenth century when the works belonged to his youngest brother, Edmund Sharpe. Thomas had gained a reputation for high-class work – Rockingham ware, buff, mottled and black lustre ware, and Derbyshire ironstone yellow ware – but after his death, when the business was carried on by his brothers, sanitary pottery rapidly became a lucrative line, and by the end of the century it was Sharpe

Brothers' speciality. Until very recent years the business was maintained under the 'Sharpe Bros' name; now there is a preservation order on the old kiln which stands adjacent to the newly-laid out shopping area.

Since Edmund Davenport's day there have been administrative and legal changes which could have facilitated the hearing of his case. In 1875 the courts of common law and Chancery were amalgamated under one supreme Court of Justice, equal powers being given to each division. No longer would Edmund Davenport need to start a separate action in order to obtain discovery of documents or to apply for an injunction. The court in which his main action commenced would have power to grant these facilities, and solicitors on either side would be expected to exchange documents before the case came to a hearing. Such delaying tactics as Edmund Davenport experienced would be unacceptable, and the present-day legal aid scheme (which provides funds whereby counsel acting for the poor man can be paid) would give him a more-nearly equal opportunity with his opponent. Today, both protagonists could go into the witness box and speak for themselves.

Winterbottom, too, might have gained from twentieth century reforms in the criminal law. In 1907 a Court of Criminal Appeal was created, and he could have had his case reconsidered by the Lord Chief Justice sitting with two other judges. Today this court has become merged with the Court of Appeal and machinery exists for an appeal against conviction, or against the sentence. Winterbottom might have had good grounds for an appeal against the severity of his sentence.

There are no prisons for debtors now. Popular opinion of the nineteenth century was turning more and more against the system, and imprisonment for debt was only allowed to continue because people thought it provided a guarantee for the granting of credit. Bills for the abolition of imprisonment for debt were introduced into Parliament during Edmund Davenport's time of imprisonment, but nothing was done until 1869. The Debtors' Act of that year abolished 'the extravagant power of the creditor' and substituted 'the calm judgment of a Judge'.[5] In other words, imprisonment for debt, as such, was abolished; in future debtors could only be punished as

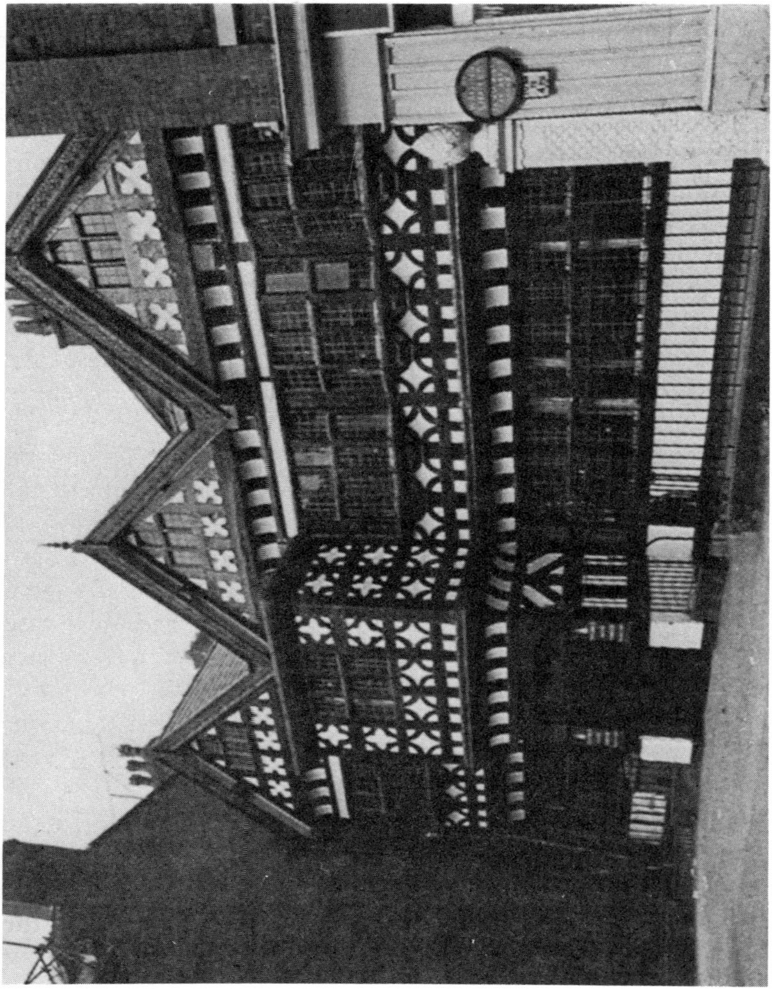

Underbank Hall: the restored facade (*National Westminster Bank PLC*)

offenders. Those buildings in which Edmund Davenport was so long confined became redundant and they have gone for ever. The Fleet Prison was closed when all its inmates had been duly transferred to the Queen's Prison, and not long afterwards it was sold (by the Commissioners of Woods and Forests!) to the Corporation of London. In 1872, following the demolition of the old prison and the completion of the new Farringdon Street and Holburn Viaduct scheme, a Congregational Memorial Hall was built upon the site. Outside the present hall, erected one hundred years later, is a notice reminding passers-by that here was the site of the Fleet Prison. The old King's (Queen's) Bench Prison at the corner of Borough Road and Southwark Bridge Road became redundant in its turn, less than forty years after it had received its face-lift as the new 'Queen's Prison'. Its later use was for military prisoners, but in 1880 it was abandoned and pulled down. Modern houses and flats now occupy the site. The Whitecross Street Prison suffered a similar fate immediately after the passing of the 1869 Debtors' Act. When that Act came into force one minute after midnight on 1 January 1870 the exodus of released prisoners from Whitecross Street commenced, too late by over fourteen years for Edmund Davenport. Some of those freed were met by friends and relations; all were watched by reporters. 'There is that shabby mildewy appearance among many which is so suggestive of such places', said one, 'and they look as though debt and difficulty were their destiny'.[6] Fifty five years after it had opened, the Whitecross Street Prison closed, and the following year (1871) the badly-planned building was demolished and the Midland Railway Company acquired the site for its extensive goods depot. For a further seventy years the place remained grim in outlook, though useful in purpose; then in the 1950s commenced the imaginative redevelopment of a now war-ravaged and desolate area. In post-war years has arisen the Barbican, the new housing development for the City of London, with its Arts Centre, its lake, its museum, and, at its centre, its old church of St Giles. That part of the lake just north of the church covers the site of the Whitecross Street Prison, and here the spirit of Edmund Davenport speaks most clearly to our consciences.

There is no transportation for forgery now, nor for any other felony. Even before John Kenyon Winterbottom was transported the system had been strongly condemned by a Select Committee of the House of Commons. 'Transportation', it said, 'is not merely inefficient in producing the moral reformation of an offender; it is efficient in demoralising those whom accidental circumstances, more than a really vicious nature, have seduced into crime'.[7] Britain was realising she must keep her criminals, and attempt their reclamation within her own shores. The concept of imprisonment was changing. For centuries prison had been looked upon primarily as a place of custody; a place to keep offenders awaiting trial and a place to keep debtors who would not (or could not) pay. Except for a minority of short custodial sentences, punishment was something different, and reformation did not enter into consideration. Felons were either hanged or (later) transported and those found guilty of lesser offences were fined, whipped or put in the stocks. The building of Millbank as a state 'penitentiary' marked a change in thinking.

As a penitentiary Millbank had not been a success. As a depot for transports it was soon out of date and became again an expensive white elephant. For the last twenty years of its life it was used as a military prison and then, in 1890, it was taken down. During the final decade of the nineteenth century Sir Henry Tate acquired the site for the picture gallery which he was giving to the nation, and the Tate Gallery, with additions over the years and substantial repairs and renovations after the Second World War, gives the place a happier aspect today.

After the terror on Norfolk Island in the summer of 1846 Major Childs was recalled, and a new superintendent sent out to restore order by stern discipline. By 1847 the Government had virtually decided to abandon the island as a penal settlement, but no decisive action was taken for seven more years. In any case transportation was now one of the main political issues within the Australian colonies themselves, and it was really only a matter of time before the whole system must be given up. In 1854 removal of the convicts from Norfolk Island commenced, and by 1856 the island was uninhabited. It was then offered by Queen Victoria to the Pitcairn Islanders – descendants of the mutineers from the *Bounty* – and nearly two hundred of them were helped by the British Government to re-settle in Norfolk

Island. Their descendants form the nucleus of the eighteen hundred or so people who today live on that beautiful island. There is now access by air, and tourists fly in to see the ruins of the convict settlement, many of which have been restored in recent years by the Australian Government. There is still no harbour, and goods coming by sea must be towed in on lighters when the weather is favourable.

In 1855 transportation to Van Diemen's Land ceased and the following year – the year in which John Kenyon Winterbottom obtained his conditional pardon – the name of the island was changed to Tasmania and a system of responsible government was introduced, laying the foundation for a free and independent people. By the beginning of the twentieth century the colony of Tasmania had become one of the six member states to unite in forming the Commonwealth of Australia. Among its many fine buildings the state capital, Hobart, still numbers its Italian-style town hall, that building which, when new, offered Winterbottom his second chance to obtain honourable recognition, and which is still in use today.

Let us return to the hamlet of Woodhouses, the place where this enquiry began. It is an elusive spot, hidden within the eastern part of the Manchester conurbation, and though it has long since become a fair-sized village it retains much of its rural character. The river Medlock, which lower down its course carried all the refuse and dirt of Manchester, was always clear and lovely here, and not long after Will Davenport's day the northern part of its valley became immortalised by Ben Brierley under the name of 'Daisy Nook'. The valley then became a special attraction as a day out for the many admirers of Brierley's sketches of Lancashire folk. Now it has become a country park, part-owned by the National Trust and preserved for the benefit of the public as 'a rural oasis in an industrial area'. At the lower end of the village of Woodhouses, overlooking Medlock Vale to the south of Daisy Nook, Robert Andrew's old farmhouse still stands. Its little group of surrounding buildings have gone, a modern bungalow has been built in the garden and part of the house itself has been taken down for road widening, but it is still a home. No Stansfields live there now, but the room where the Stansfield ladies kept their shop and the room above where Rob Andrew stored Will

Robert Andrew's farmhouse, c.1980 (*Estate of the late Miss Agnes Stansfield*)

Davenport's letters form part of the surviving building. As I drive slowly past (the road is still narrow for motor traffic) I reflect on the way that a bundle of old letters can start a trail leading one vividly back to the hopes, fears and tragedies of persons in the long-forgotten past.

SOURCES AND NOTES TO THE CHAPTERS

I THE MEETING TIME

This chapter is a reconstruction from the *Woodhouses Letters* with additional information taken from parish registers or supplied by Miss Agnes Stansfield.

1 Note in George Webster's handwriting, unaddressed and unsigned.
2 John Swindells to George Webster, 9 September 1839.
3 This letter is undated and unsigned, but a letter in another hand dated January 1840 shows that someone was then considering Richard's case. Most of the back page of the second letter, including the signature, is so ingrained with dust as to be illegible, perhaps indicating that it was kept on top of the pile.

II IMPRISONMENT FOR DEBT: the case of Edmund Davenport (1)

For the history of the Davenport family of Bramhall see J.P. Earwaker, *East Cheshire: past and present* (1877), vol. 1, pp. 422–455; E. B. Dean, *Bramall Hall: the story of an Elizabethan manor house* (1977).

For synopsis of Edmund Davenport's life to date, and the outcome of his trials as related to Richard Oastler, see postcript to Oastler's *Fleet Papers*, 17 April 1841. War Office pay lists in the Public Record Office (WO12/1468–9) confirm his army service. Davenport was a private during the 1798 Irish fighting, being promoted to corporal on passage to Egypt.

The Bill of Discovery in the Public Record Office (C13/2656) gives information concerning Edmund Davenport's claimed pedigree, and Chancery orders chart his fate, see C33/814–2803 (1831); C33/824–387 (1832); C33/826–917 (1832); C33/857–395 (1833); C33/859–1359 (1834); C33/864–57 (1834).

For reports of Hulme's case see *Chester Chronicle,* 3 April 1835; *Stockport Advertiser,* 3 April 1835; also letter, John Ham to Hugh

Knowles, 2 April 1835.

The *Woodhouses Letters* form the major source for the narrative of this chapter. In particular, the letters of John Ham to Hugh Knowles (1834–5) record Edmund Davenport's attempts to make an entry on the Bramhall estate, though naturally there are gaps in the story as Ham's letters only form one side of the correspondence. I have been unable to discover exactly who John Ham was, although one or two persons of that name are mentioned in London directories of the time. Words flowed freely from his pen, and he seems suited to the position of a clerk. At the beginning of 1835 he wrote that he was 'up to the eyes' in the elections, presumably referring to the parliamentary elections which preceded Peel's short ministry of three months.

No official records of Edmund Davenport's ejectment trial appear now to be in existence, many of the Chester assize records having been lost long before it was officially decided to transfer them to the Public Record Office. However, a full report of the trial appeared in the *Chester Chronicle*, 21 August 1835, and shorter reports in the local Stockport and district papers. All quotations are taken from the *Chester Chronicle*. The extract from the speech of Mr Temple, leading counsel for Edmund Davenport, given in the *Chester Chronicle* agrees with that copied by George Webster and printed at the beginning of this chapter, except that Webster's version is in direct speech, the other in indirect. One would assume that Webster had access to an actual draft of the speech.

1 The story is told in P. Wentworth, *The history and annals of Blackley and neighbourhood* (1892), pp. 39–42.
2 The name has been spelled in various ways over the centuries, the form for the place being fixed in the late nineteenth century as 'Bramhall'. When the Hazel Grove & Bramhall Urban District Council purchased the Hall and Park in 1935 they chose to call the building 'Bramall Hall', following the earlier form.
3 See Owen MSS, vol. 26, pp. 63–4 (in Manchester Reference Library); Burton MSS, *Bramhall*, vol. 1, The manor, pp. 495 & 496 (held by the Stockport Metropolitan Borough Council); *Fleet Papers*, 17 April 1841.
4 See R. C. Davenport, *A brief account of the Davenports of east Cheshire and a branch therefrom* (1899).
5 *Fleet Papers*, 17 April 1841.
6 6 April 1832. This letter to James Davenport must have been penned for Edmund by someone else, although up to the end of 1835 his letters seem usually to be in his own hand. The letter concludes: 'I may add that my friends here has never wished for any agreement, though of course, if I am successful they will be handsomely rewarded'. Perhaps it was written for Edmund by one

of the 'friends' he mentions. The handwriting is remarkably like that of Peter Morrison, who comes into the story a little later, and wrote business letters on Edmund's behalf.

7 Peter Morrison to Joseph Lomas, 4 April 1834.
8 Thomas Sharpe to Joseph Lomas, 4 June 1834.
9 25 November 1834.
10 26 November (1834).
11 30 November (1834).
12 John Ham to Hugh Knowles, 11 December 1834.
13 Chapter 41, from which quotations are taken.
14 John Ham to Hugh Knowles, 30 January 1835.
15 John Ham to Hugh Knowles, 20 May 1835.
16 The title of Edmund Davenport's ejectment case – Doe d. (on the demise of) Davenport versus Humphreys – may puzzle some readers. The story of Doe and Roe was a fiction used by the legal profession and accepted by the courts in order to avoid the mediaeval paraphernalia of the land law and adapt for the freeholder a remedy (the action of ejectment) which was technically only available to the leaseholder. The real plaintiff (the man who claimed the freehold) declared that he had demised the disputed land to a man called John Doe. Doe, so it was said, entered and took possession of the land, only to be turned out by another person, Richard Roe, the 'casual ejector'. Doe, as leaseholder, was entitled to bring a case against Roe, but the latter now disappeared from the scene leaving the real possessor to defend the case for him. The courts always insisted that the real defender must be given due notice, otherwise there was a danger that the case could go against him by default. The case then became a straightforward trial of the title of the 'lessor of the plaintiff' (the man who said he had made the lease, in this case Edmund Davenport) as against the title of the man in possession (Sir Salusbury Pryce Humphreys).

The whole of this totally false story was told on every declaration in ejectment. The procedure was abolished by the Common Law Procedure Act of 1852, when a simple action became possible.

17 Until 1845, when a simple deed of conveyance became possible, transfer of freehold property was usually made by deeds of lease and release, thus avoiding the Statute of Enrolments (1535) which provided that any transfer of freehold land by 'bargain and sale' must be enrolled on the court records. A lease took away actual possession of the land in favour of a tenant, but possession would still legally revert to the owner when the period of lease was over. It was legally possible to 'release' (surrender) this reversion to the tenant, thus making him in effect a freeholder, and thus the

business could be effected without publicity. During the nineteenth century there was much agitation over the secrecy involved in the transfer of land, and various suggestions concerning the registration of either titles or deeds were brought before Parliament.

18 *Pickwick Papers*, ch. 41.

19 This is Edmund's spelling. It is an earlier variant of his surname, but none of his contemporaries used this form.

20 William Davenport's deeds of lease and release are now deposited in the Cheshire Record Office (DDA/1384/201/14–15). The lease, to Thomas William Tatton, is signed and sealed by William Davenport and witnessed by Will Sergeant (a solicitor in Manchester), John Hallworth and William Orme (William Davenport's butler). The release, made the following day and containing the real conditions of the conveyance, is signed and sealed by both parties and witnessed on William Davenport's behalf by the same three people. They also witnessed his will which confirmed these deeds. Any person who had access to the will but not to the deeds of lease and release would know that some disposition of property had been made, but they would be ignorant of its exact nature.

The documents appear perfectly in order, and they must have passed legal scrutiny when the estate was sold.

III TRANSPORTATION FOR FORGERY: the case of John Kenyon Winterbottom (1)

Background information concerning the borough of Stockport in the early nineteenth century and John Kenyon Winterbottom's career before 1840 can be found in the files of the *Stockport Advertiser*, and in H. Heginbotham, *Stockport ancient and modern* (2 vols. 1882 & 1892). There are reports of J. K. Winterbottom's bankruptcy, supposed frauds, abscondment, capture, trial and sentencing in the Stockport and Manchester papers and in *The Times*. The hearing of his reserved legal points is reported in 1 DEN 41–51 and 2 CAR & K 37–47. Davenport solicitor accounts in the Cheshire Record Office (DDA/1533/31) cast light on the behind-the-scenes activities of Sir Salusbury Davenport's new solicitors, Messrs Lingard & Vaughan. For the voyage of the *Mayda* to Norfolk Island see *Journal of HM Convict Ship Mayda 1845–6* in the Public Record Office (ADM/101/52/5).

1 Heginbotham, vol. 1, p. 170.

2 Letter to the *Stockport Advertiser*, 20 April 1832.

3 'Herculean' was the adjective used by the *Stockport Advertiser* on 13 September 1844 in its appeal for a more charitable view of Winterbottom's case than that taken by some newspapers.
4 Printed in all accounts of the trial.
5 *Stockport Advertiser,* 14 August 1840, editorial article 'Mr Winterbottom's bankruptcy'.
6 Cheshire Record Office, DDA/1533/31, 29 August 1840; 15 September 1840.
7 ibid., 2 October 1841.
8 *The Times,* 9 September 1844, copying the *Manchester Guardian.*
9 7 December 1844.
10 Sir George Head, *A home tour through the manufacturing districts of England in the summer of 1835* (1836), p.59.
11 *Stockport Advertiser,* morning edition, 6 December 1844. The newspaper had been obliged to go into print before the result of the trial was known, and therefore brought out a second edition later the same day, which included a long report of the trial, as well as giving a repeat report the following week. Quotations from Mr Jervis's speech for the defence are taken from the second edition, 6 December 1844.
12 *The Times,* 7 December 1844.
13 1 DEN 51.
14 *The Times,* 3 April 1845.
15 *Stockport Advertiser,* 4 April 1845.
16 For record of his stay here see PRO PCOM/2/24, *Millbank Prison Register.*
17 For first-hand accounts of Norfolk Island at this time see J. F. Mortlock, *Experiences of a convict,* ed. by G. A. Wilkes and A. G. Mitchell (Sydney, 1965); *Household Words,* 10 April 1852, 31 July and 7 August 1852.

IV IMPRISONMENT FOR DEBT: the case of Edmund Davenport (2)

There are longer gaps in the *Woodhouses Letters* after 1840 and they end in 1846. Taking their place as a major source for the continuation of Edmund Davenport's story (though from the opposite point of view) are the Davenport of Bramhall solicitors' accounts from 31 July 1840 to 17 May 1849 (DDA/1533/31) which are deposited in the Cheshire Record Office.

Chancery orders showing the results of Edmund Davenport's various petitions, and recording the final attachments issued against him, are in the Public Record Office, see C33/913 (1842); C33/919 (1843); C33/920 (1843); C33/943 (1845); C33/971 (1848); C33/980

(1849); C33/981 (1849). For Edmund Davenport's second Chancery bill see PRO C14/965.

The coroner's inquisition taken on Edmund Davenport's death, together with the depositions of three witnesses and the names of the jury, is in the City of London Record Office, Guildhall.

1 A letter dated 18 April 1840 from Sir Salusbury's London agents warned the warden of the Fleet that he would be held responsible for any surreptitious or unauthorised discharge of Edmund Davenport of which Sir Salusbury was not cognisant. The letter is inserted in the Fleet Committal Book against the record of Edmund Davenport (PRO PRIS/1/46).

2 *Fleet Papers,* 26 November 1842.
In this article the value of the 'paternal estate' is over-estimated at £6000 per annum. A Cheshire Record Office document (DDA/1384/197A/22) of probably late nineteenth century date shows the annual rental of the Bramhall estate to be a little over £4000. Richard Davenport (or George Webster) also vastly over-estimated the value, mentioning 'the Prize of ten thousand', but it could not have been easy for any outsider to obtain accurate figures.

3 *The Jurist,* vol. 6, pp. 633–5.
See also 1 PH 124–9; *The Times,* 21 July 1842; *Law Reports* XX, n.s. XI, Chancery, 325–7.
The argument as to whether a person suing *in forma pauperis* could be kept in prison for any costs whatsoever was of interest to the legal profession generally and therefore widely reported.

4 Declarations in ejectment were served on Sir Salusbury himself and on various groups of tenants, but Sir Salusbury had to defend them all. An affidavit of service on Robert Sharp at Bramall Hall is in the Public Record Office (KB/101/13/30). The story of Doe and Roe is *printed* on the other side of the affidavit, the blank spaces being filled in by hand with the names of Edmund Davenport and Robert Chapman Sharp and a description of the property concerned. E. Turner, Edmund Davenport's representative, called at Bramall Hall on 21 October 1842, delivered the declaration to William Jenkinson, a servant (presumably because Sharp was not there), and read it over and explained it to him. A few days later Turner called again to obtain an acknowledgment.

5 Edmund Davenport to John Wild, 3 November 1845.

6 This letter is the only one of the *Woodhouses Letters* written to a member of Edmund Davenport's immediate family. Neither the address nor the married name of his daughter is given. The letter mentions 'Joseph' and 'Thomas' (perhaps sons-in-law) and 'my Grandchildren'. It is not surprising that most of Edmund's letters

seem to be to people nearer Will Davenport, if Will was in fact the originator of the collection.

7 A 'fine' or 'final concord' was a compromised case brought by two parties in collusion with the object of establishing the title of one of them to land, and it could be used to effect a family settlement. Fines which concerned land within the county palatine of Chester were enrolled in the court at Chester, and these fines are now at the Public Record Office. There is a fine of October 1656 which seems to form part of a 'common recovery with double voucher' (another fictitious action), passing seisin or possession of the Bramhall estate to Thomas Legh and Edward Hyde. This action would have the effect of barring any previous entail to which the Bramhall estate might be subject and paving the way for a new settlement. One would then expect Thomas Legh and Edward Hyde to grant back the lands to Peter Davenport for life, with remainder to his male heirs, but of such a deed I can find no trace. The whole procedure seems unbelievably clumsy and complicated, but because the resulting settlement would be made with the approval of the court it could be expected to be upheld by the court, and in the 1650s – the period of Commonwealth and Protectorate – this was a very important consideration.

8 PRO C14/965 (1849 D.No. 12).

9 7 HARE 217–224.
See also *The Jurist*, 1849, pt. 1, pp. 227–9; *Law Journal*, Chancery, n.s. vol. 18, pt. 2, pp. 163–4.

10 See Cheshire Record Office DDA/1384/203/7 for Maria Davenport's preparations and Public Record Office ASSI 57/4 p. 38 for official record of withdrawal.

The trustees of Jonathan Hardcastle held 'the several deeds and writings' of a substantial part of the Bramhall estate as security for mortgage, and on 31 March 1849 Richard Sykes, the second trustee, took away the deeds from the office of the Hardcastle solicitors for the purpose of producing them at a trial at the current Chester assizes. He gave a receipt at the bottom of the mortgage documents (DDA/1384/203/7). His receipt has been crossed through, showing that the deeds were returned. He took them again on 2 August 1849 for the purpose of producing them at the 'now ensuing Chester assizes', but in neither case was the production of the deeds of the Bramhall estate necessary.

11 *Report from the committee on the King's Bench, Fleet and Marshalsea Prisons &c*, p. 28.

12 *The London Prisons*, pp. 279, 280.

13 ibid. p. 281.

14 by 'Clyde' (pseud. of D. G. Porter).

V TRANSPORTATION FOR FORGERY: the case of John Kenyon Winterbottom (2)

Information concerning the overseas record of John Kenyon Winterbottom, which forms the basis of this chapter, has been supplied by the Archives Office of Tasmania.

1 *The London Prisons*, p. 278.
2 J. F. Mortlock, op. cit., p. 84.
3 The details of the charge against him and account of the trial are taken from *The Mercury*, Hobart, 11 September 1867. All quotations are from *The Mercury*.

VI THEN AND NOW

1 Abstract of title of J. W. H. Davenport. Cheshire Record Office, DDA/1384/203/5–6.
2 13 August 1832.
This seems to be a copy of a letter from Edmund Davenport. It is written from 8 Spencer Street, Northampton Square, London, as is another letter of this period, and it is addressed to 'friends'. Although the letter is unsigned, the contents leave no doubt that it is from Edmund.
3 *Stockport ancient and modern*, vol. 2, p. 265.
4 *Stockport Advertiser*, 13 September 1844.
5 *Illustrated Times*, 8 January 1870.
6 *The Graphic*, 15 January 1870.
7 Report of the Molesworth Committee on transportation, 1838.

INDEX